DAILY LIFE IN
VICTORIAN ENGLAND

THE HORIZON BOOK OF
DAILY LIFE IN VICTORIAN ENGLAND

by Christopher Hibbert

Published by AMERICAN HERITAGE PUBLISHING CO., INC., New York

Book Trade Distribution by McGRAW-HILL BOOK COMPANY

Library of Congress Cataloging in Publication Data
Hibbert, Christopher, 1924–
    The Horizon book of daily life in Victorian England.
    (Daily life in five great ages of history)
    Bibliography: p. 126
    Includes index.
    1. England—Social life and customs—19th century.
I. Title. II. Title: Daily life in Victorian England.
III. Series.
DA533.H5   942.081   75–16272
ISBN 0–07–028657–4

Contents

I   The Upper Class   4

II   Belowstairs   18

III   The Middle Class   28

IV   Growing Up   40

V   Country Life   54

VI   Workers   66

VII   By the Railway   78

VIII   On Holiday   88

IX   The Underworld   102

X   Flesh and the Spirit   112

Acknowledgments   126

Bibliography   126

Index   127

4046

1837 1897

THE DIAMOND JUBILEE

CHAPTER I

THE UPPER CLASS

One summer day toward the end of the last century, a nervous eighteen-year-old American heiress, Consuelo Vanderbilt, was driven to Blenheim Palace in Oxfordshire. She was going to spend a long English weekend with her mother as a guest of the ninth duke of Marlborough, whom it was intended that she should soon marry.

"We entered the park through a stone arch," she later recorded. "A porter in livery carrying a long wand surmounted by a silver knob from which hung a red cord and tassel stood at attention and the great house loomed in the distance. At the right of us and below lay an ornamental lake spanned by a monumental bridge. We turned into a fine avenue of elms and passed through another arch leading into a court. . . . A flight of shallow steps led up to the main entrance of the Palace. The doors opened onto an immense hall with a domed ceiling."

Miss Vanderbilt was led across the grandiose hall, past a painting of the Great Duke clothed in a Roman toga and driving a chariot, toward the Great Saloon, where there were further memorials to her host's ancestor, this time frescoes

JAMES LAVER, Victoriana, 1966

painted by Laguerre. "Drawing rooms stretched in vistas on either side of the Saloon," in which, beneath "two impressive mantelpieces, a tea table had been set." After a while the duke appeared, an opinionated, disdainful young man with "a small aristocratic face with a large nose and rather prominent blue eyes. His hands, which he used in a fastidious manner, were well shaped and he seemed inordinately proud of them." The evening was spent listening to the duke's organist in the Long Library, and the next morning His Grace took his guests on a drive through "the outlying villages [of his estate], where old women and children curtsied and men touched their caps as we passed."

The Blenheim estate extended to nearly 24,000 acres, from which the duke derived an income of £37,000 a year (the equivalent of $180,042 at a time when the pound was worth $4.86). Enormous as this sum was when income tax was only a few pence on the pound, Marlborough was not a rich man compared with some other members of his class. The marquis of Bute's estate brought him about £150,000 a year, the duke of Northumberland's £176,000, the duke of Devonshire's £181,000, and the duke of Buccleuch's £217,000. The duke of Westminster enjoyed an annual income of £250,000 from his London property alone, and the duke of Bedford, so Disraeli informed the queen, had an

Victoria had been queen of England for sixty years when the souvenir on the opposite page, showing the monarch in her youth, was issued for the Diamond Jubilee. The mother-of-pearl fan above is a treasured memento of her era.

income "absolutely exceeding £300,000." Nor was the duke of Marlborough's landed estate large in comparison with many others. There were over forty landowners who owned more than 100,000 acres. The duke of Buccleuch had 460,000; and the duke of Sutherland 1,358,000, an area larger than the counties of Bedfordshire, Berkshire, and Buckinghamshire put together.

The less rich of these landed aristocrats required constant infusions of money if they were to live in the style to which their upbringing had accustomed them, and several found the necessary money by marrying wealthy wives. Lord Rosebery chose a Rothschild; the eighth duke of Marlborough, divorced by his first wife, chose as his second an immensely wealthy American widow, Mrs. Hammersley; the ninth duke, although in love at the time with someone else, decided that he could not find a more suitable consort than the great-granddaughter of Cornelius Vanderbilt.

Consuelo Vanderbilt herself was not much taken with the idea. And after a dispiriting honeymoon, she began her life as mistress of Blenheim Palace with trepidation. She arrived at Woodstock by special train, then walked on a red carpet from the station to a carriage, from which the horses had been unhitched so that the duke's employees could drag her to the palace to the acclamations of the assembled tenants. As she stood on the steps listening to the various speeches of welcome, weighed down by her heavy fur coat, her arms full of bouquets, her big hat blown about by the wind, the new duchess "suddenly felt distraught." Nor did her early experiences of life in an aristocratic palace reconcile her to a daily existence with a fastidious, sarcastic husband to whom she felt increasingly antipathetic. That first day on which she entered Blenheim as his wife, her maid was

The conservatory with its potted palms and comfortable furniture was the scene of afternoon gatherings, like this one painted by James Tissot.

waiting for her in her room; a tea gown of satin and lace was laid out, and she dressed for the "ritual of dinner such as Marlborough, the chef and the butler had decreed it to be":

How I learned to dread and hate these dinners, how ominous and wearisome they loomed at the end of a long day. They were served with all the accustomed ceremony, but once a course had been passed the servants retired to the hall; the door was closed and only a ring of the bell placed before Marlborough summoned them. He had a way of piling food on his plate; the next move was to push the plate away, together with knives, forks, spoons and glasses—all this in considered gestures which took a long time; then he backed his chair away from the table, crossed one leg over the other and endlessly twisted the ring on his little finger. . . . After a quarter of an hour he would suddenly return to earth or perhaps I should say to food and begin to eat very slowly, usually complaining that the food was cold! . . . As a rule neither of us spoke a word. I took to knitting in desperation and the butler read detective stories in the hall.

The duchess found that large dinner parties at Blenheim were scarcely more endurable. In the first place they entailed a great deal of preliminary worry, for the duke was highly critical of the slightest mismanagement. Indeed, the whole arrangement of a weekend house party was an extremely trying business. First there were the invitations to issue to twenty-five or thirty guests; then the discussions with the butler and the chef, who were not only jealous of each other but perpetually complaining of the misdemeanors of their underlings; then the inspections of the guest rooms with the housekeeper to insure that they contained all that would be required—hot- and cold-water jugs, soap and sponge bowls, towels and mats, and, in particular, bathtubs in front of the fires—for Blenheim, like most other noblemen's houses, contained only one or two bathrooms. Most worrying of all were the arrangements for the procession of guests into the dining room and for their seating around the table, since the rules of precedence had to be rigidly followed. This the duchess discovered immediately after her first big dinner party when one earl crossly complained that his superiority over another had not been recognized as it should have been.

Victorian elegance of dress reached its peak in garden parties at the turn of the century.

During the dinner there was constant anxiety that the eight-course meal would not be completed within the hour that the duke stipulated as being a sufficient time in which to consume it, an undertaking rendered all the more difficult by the kitchen being a good three hundred yards from the dining room and by there usually being at least one greedy guest, who, unable to choose between the dishes offered him, wanted to have a taste of everything available.

The amount of food laid upon the dinner table in such houses as Blenheim was prodigious. First there would be a choice of soups, clear or thick, hot or cold; then two kinds of fish, poached turbot, say, and salmon mayonnaise. Two removes—turkey and roast mutton, perhaps—would accompany several entrées, such as cutlets, *vol-au-vent*, fillets of leveret, or sautéed fillets of fowl, served before two roasts. There might come a sorbet and after that, in the shooting season, the game course—partridge, pheasant, duck, woodcock, and snipe. When there was no game, quail and ortolan were shipped over from the Continent. There would also be numerous entremets—lobster salad, maraschino jelly, truffles with champagne.

The method of serving this succulent fare varied from house to house. The old-fashioned preferred to retain the eighteenth-century practice of having several dishes on the table at once, the gentlemen helping themselves once the covers had been removed, offering to help their neighbors, and sending a servant to fetch anything they could not reach. In other houses service was *à la russe*, each course being served separately and handed round by servants in white gloves, who either offered the dishes first to the ladies and then to the gentlemen or went straight round the table from one guest to the next.

"At the conclusion of the second course comes a sort of intermediate dessert of cheese, butter, salad, raw celery and the like," wrote Prince Pückler-Muskau, a German visitor to England earlier in the century:

after which, ale, sometimes thirty or forty years old, and so strong that when thrown on the fire it blazes like spirit, is handed about. The table-cloth is then removed: under it, at the best tables, is a finer, upon which the dessert is set. At the inferior ones it is placed on the bare polished table. It consists of all sorts of hothouse fruits . . . confitures, and the like.

Clean glasses are set before every guest, and, with the dessert plates and knives and forks, small fringed napkins are laid. Three decanters are usually placed before the master of the house, generally containing claret, port, and sherry, or madeira. The host pushes these in stands, or in a little silver waggon on wheels, to his neighbour on the left. Every man pours out his own wine, and if a lady sits next to him, also helps her. . . . It is not usual to take wine without drinking to another person. When you raise your glass, you look fixedly at the one with whom you are drinking, bow your head, and then drink with great gravity. . . . It is esteemed a civility to invite anybody in this way to drink; and a messenger is often sent from one end of the table to another.

During this toasting and drinking all the servants left the room, and about a quarter of an hour later, the hostess "collected eyes" and led the ladies out also. In the eighteenth century the men had stayed drinking, often until they

Boar's head with aspic jelly
CHARLES E. FRANCATELLI, *The Modern Cook*, 1862

Three-tiered mold of game mousse
CHARLES RANHOFER, *The Epicurean*, 1920

Galantine de Dinde à la Volière
ALEXIS SOYER, *The Gastronomic Regenerator*, 1852

Surrounding this picture of a formal dinner are elegant

were all quite drunk; but the queen's example at Court was now followed in most upper-class houses, and the men, having had coffee, would shortly follow the ladies to the drawing room, where tea awaited them.

Although dinner was, of course, the most elaborate meal of the day, the amount and variety of food offered at other meals were scarcely less abundant. The breakfasts served at Plumstead Episcopi were not products of Anthony Trollope's imagination: many well-to-do Victorians *did* come downstairs to "dry toast and buttered toast, muffins and crumpets; hot bread and cold bread, home-made bread, baker's bread, wheaten bread and oaten bread . . . eggs in napkins and crispy bits of bacon under silver covers . . . and little fishes . . . and devilled kidneys frizzling on a hot-water dish."

In the middle of the morning there would be a glass of wine and cake and biscuits for those who could not wait for luncheon, and in the afternoon there would be tea for those who could not wait for dinner. In the earlier years of the queen's reign, tea was merely cups of tea, as the actress Fanny Kemble discovered during a visit to the duke of Rutland's castle at Belvoir, where the duchess of Bedford was a fellow guest. "I received on several occasions private and rather mysterious invitations to the duchess of Bedford's room," wrote Fanny Kemble, "and found her with a 'small and select' circle of female guests, busily employed in brewing and drinking tea, with her grace's own private tea-kettle. I do not believe that now universally honored and observed institution of 'five-o'clock tea' dates farther back in the annals of English civilization than this very private and, I think, rather shamefaced, practice of it."

articles that could be expected to appear on the table.

Helmet made of ice cream
CHARLES RANHOFER, *The Epicurean*, 1920

Dessert topped with a figure of Bacchus
CHARLES RANHOFER, *The Epicurean*, 1920

Serving utensils
Illustrated London News, JULY 26, 1851

Thirty years after these slightly secretive meetings in the duchess of Bedford's room, tea was fashionable all over England, and with each passing decade, more and more food was eaten with it: at first very thin bread and butter, then biscuits, then cake, and, finally, a variety of muffins, scones, sandwiches, and assorted buns and shortbreads, a proper meal, in fact, for which ladies changed into tea gowns.

Tea was no sooner over than it was time to change for dinner. Changing clothes, indeed, occupied a large part of the lady's day. She might appear at breakfast in her riding habit, but otherwise each meal required its own particular costume. And putting on this costume was a lengthy process, for the flimsy, figure-revealing—often transparent—frocks of the Regency had long since given way to dresses of an increasingly cumbersome, figure-concealing fussiness. In the 1830's a footman in the employment of a rich widow confided to his diary how deeply the immodest clothes of his mistress's young guests shocked his sense of propriety. "It's quite disgusting to the modist eye to see the way the young ladies dress to attract the notice of the gentlemen," he wrote. "They are nearly naked to the waist, only just a little bit of dress hanging on the shoulder, the breasts are quite exposed except a little bit comeing up to hide the nipples. Plenty of false hair and teeth and paint. If a person wish to see the ways of the world, they must be a gentleman's servant, then they mite see it to perfection."

This footman died in 1892, and by then he had no cause for such complaints. False hair and teeth were still employed, but a painted face was seen only on the stage or in those establishments in Haymarket from whose very doors the eyes of respectable ladies were averted. In the 1880's Sarah Bernhardt appeared in polite society with white powder on her face and a kohllike make-up to emphasize her eyes. But actresses were permitted a certain license that would never have been extended to ladies; and it was another actress, Ellen Terry, who noted how "astonishing" it seemed when Bernhardt, "while talking to [Henry Irving], took some red stuff out of her bag and rubbed it on her lips."

If a real lady wanted to use cosmetics, she had to do so with such discretion that the effects appeared to be only the slightest improvement upon nature. Lip salves, containing a hint of carmine, might perhaps be used by those with the excuse of a chapped skin; and rich and daring ladies might secretly visit some such establishment as Madame Rachel's in New Bond Street, where "Chinese Leaves for the Cheeks and Lips," "Magnetic Rock Dew Water of the Sahara," "Venus's Toilet," and similar preparations were offered for sale at prices commensurate with the magical ingredients that they were alleged to contain. But most gentlewomen, nervous of being detected in some unseemly artifice, had to be content with soap and water, sponge and brush, to bring the contrast of color to a pale face.

Yet, if the Victorian lady, unlike her grandmother, spent little time in applying make-up to her face, she—or her maid—took a great deal of time in dressing her hair. It was combed and brushed, polished and plaited, then coiled into an elaborate knob at the back of her neck; or, during the last two decades of the century, it was brushed forward from the back of the head, in what was known as the French fashion, then coiled into an equally elaborate mass on top. And since this new style rendered it impossible for hats to be secured in place by a piece of elastic running under the old-fashioned bun, long pins came into use to be driven through the hat and hair and to add to the impedimenta that every well-dressed gentlewoman required.

The most tiresome and restricting of these impedimenta were corsets, which even young girls wore to compress their waists to the desired dimension of eighteen inches and which were frequently responsible for fainting fits and occasionally for permanent ill-health. Some ladies dispensed with corsets when going out riding, but many did not; and all wore other clothes sufficiently cumbersome to make the abscence of a corset little relief. Cloth trousers and voluminous petticoats would be covered by full skirts that almost reached the ground. Hands were encased in gauntlets; heads crowned by a hat from whose lining descended a veil. For less active pursuits even more muffling clothes were worn. In the late 1840's the crinoline was foreshadowed by the air-tube dress

Tissot's painting The Ball on Shipboard *is believed to depict a dance aboard the royal yacht at Cowes during Regatta week.*

extender; and by the late 1850's the crinoline had firmly established itself, remaining in fashion, disliked as it was, until the late 1860's. Long after the crinoline had disappeared, the bustle was still seen, and leg-of-mutton sleeves outlasted the century, as did those long, trailing skirts, which had to be held up before their wearers could move about in them. Some advanced women took to the bloomer, a short skirt with loose trousers gathered round the ankles, a form of dress recommended by the American advocate of women's rights Amelia Jenks Bloomer; but most ladies considered this sort of apparel quite shockingly outré. In any case, the bloomer both concealed and impeded female legs and knees rather than revealed their charms. Knickers began to be worn in 1890, though in a very apologetic kind of way at first, being long and wide and frilled at the edges so that if they were seen at all, they would look like the petticoats they were intended to replace. At the end of the century the customers of Harrod's, the fashionable department store, were not being offered underclothes much more liberating than these. By then a separate blouse might have been worn by a lady playing tennis; but even for this activity she still wore a long, though not a trailing, skirt, and she normally kept her corset

Henry, the seventh duke of Beaufort, sitting astride his horse in the foreground, is about to lead a hunt on the

on as well even on the hottest of summer days.

The clothes of a Victorian gentleman were scarcely more suited to his various occupations than were those of his wife and daughters until the less formal clothes required for playing games had their effect upon the dress worn at other times. A frock coat with a black waistcoat, a tall black top hat, a silk cravat, and wide tubular trousers, which touched the ground at the heel of the boot and rose over the instep in front, not only were *de rigueur* in London but were also worn on certain occasions in the country. Many gentlemen, indeed, wore black frock coats even on the most informal occasions in the country: if Millais's portrait is to be believed, John Ruskin wore his when climbing mountains; and Lord Salisbury went so far as to don his for shooting rabbits. As late as the 1890's the prince of Wales could be seen riding down Rotten Row in a long coat and silk hat.

Less formal attire for other pursuits was by then, however, considered acceptable by all but the most die-hard conservative. What were to become known as sports coats and business suits were often seen in fashionable country houses in the late 1860's, when a gentleman could also walk the streets of a market town without fear of ridicule in the headgear recently put on sale

grounds of Badminton, his estate in Wiltshire. William and Henry Barraud painted this stylish scene in 1836.

by the London hatter John Bowler or, in summer, in a round, flat straw hat with a silk ribbon, known as a boater.

Although obliged to change his clothes less often than the ladies of his household, a gentleman, having put on evening dress for dinner, would then be expected to don a smoking jacket and possibly a smoking cap as well if he wanted to enjoy a cigar with a glass of brandy and water before following the ladies to bed. In early Victorian England smoking was not as widespread as it later became; and there were many members of society who strongly objected to it, though few of them as strongly as Lord Melbourne, who always made "a great row about it" and, if he smelled tobacco, "swore perhaps for half an hour." The queen also "had a rooted objection to smoking and even disliked reading letters written by anyone who had smoked when writing," according to her assistant private secretary, Sir Frederick Ponsonby. "Smoking at Windsor necessitated a very long walk for the guests, as the billiard-room, which was the only room in which smoking was allowed, was a long way off. In conceding the billiard-room to smokers the Queen thought she was really doing all that was necessary. If any gentlemen wished to indulge in the disgusting habit of smoking he should go as far away as possible."

When her third daughter, Princess Helena Victoria, married Prince Christian of Schleswig-Holstein, Queen Victoria

heard to her horror that he smoked. It was not so bad as if he drank, but still it was a distinct blemish on his otherwise impeccable character. The Queen, however, decided to be broad-minded and actually to give him a room [at Balmoral] where he could indulge in this habit. A small room was found near the servants' quarters which could only be reached by crossing the open kitchen courtyard, and in this back room was placed a wooden chair and table. She looked upon this room as a sort of opium-den.

It distressed the queen that Prince Albert was also a smoker; and although in later years she herself was once seen on a picnic in Scotland puffing at a cigarette to keep the midges away, her aversion to the practice was believed to be so extreme that when two of her sons entered her room suddenly one day to offer their condolences upon some disaster, they thought it well to apologize profusely for having dared to appear before her in their smoking jackets. Even Prince Albert did not presume to smoke in her presence; and at Osborne House, the mansion that Thomas Cubitt, with his royal master at his elbow, designed for the royal family on the Isle of Wight, a special smoking room was built, the only room with a lone *A* above the door instead of an *A* entwined with a *V*.

The smoking room at Osborne was installed in 1845; and thereafter most country houses were provided with rooms in which gentlemen could smoke and drink free from the constraints imposed by the company of ladies, if not rooms specifically devoted to the enjoyment of tobacco at least male preserves, like billiard rooms or gun rooms, which no women other than servants would normally enter. It became, indeed, unthinkable for a man of means to build a country house for himself and his family without insuring that his architect provided a male sanctuary of some size, though not often on the grand scale of Bryanston, the gigantic house designed by Norman Shaw in Dorset for Lord Portman, whose male guests could retreat from the ladies to their bachelor bedrooms through a whole series of gentlemen's apartments, from billiard room and lavatories to smoking room and sitting room.

Lord Portman came from an old family long settled in his county. So did the duke of Westminster, for whom Alfred Waterhouse rebuilt an immense Gothic family house, Eaton Hall in Cheshire, at a cost of about £600,000. The marquis of Bute, who spent even more on restoring Cardiff Castle, was also of aristocratic stock. But most country houses constructed in Queen Victoria's time were built for men, or the sons of men, who had made fortunes in banking or industry. Lord Wolverton's house at Iwerne Minster, for instance, was built with the profits of railways; Sir Arthur Wilson's Tranby Croft, with those of ships. A cotton tycoon built Orchardleigh House in Somerset, and a wool millionaire built Milner Field in Yorkshire.

It was not the aim of the newly rich to overthrow the old aristocracy, so one of them assured Hippolyte Adolphe Taine, the French critic and historian, who spent several months in England in 1859: "We are ready to leave the government and high offices in their hands. For we believe

The Countess of Montalbo and her husband John Bowes chose a French chateau as the model for their home, which they built between 1869 and 1885. Now a museum, the house still stands in the town of Barnard Castle.

. . . that the conduct of national business calls for special men, men born and bred to the work for generations, and who enjoy an independent and commanding situation. Besides, their titles and pedigree give them a quality of dash and style. . . . But we do absolutely insist that all positions of power be filled by able men. No mediocrities and no nepotism. Let them govern, but let them be fit to govern."

It was generally agreed by the rest of the nation that they *were* fit to govern. Even a radical politician like Richard Cobden felt bound to conclude that the upper classes had "never stood so high in relative social and political rank" as they did in the middle of the nineteenth century. There were still plenty of wastrels and rakes to be found among them, as the queen never tired of reminding her eldest son. Gambling ruined the last marquis of Hastings; wild prodigality led to the duke of Buckingham's amassing debts of £1,000,000 and to the enforced sale of his beautiful house at Stowe; and the careers of such flamboyant figures as the earl of Cardigan—leader of the most famous cavalry charge in history, seducer of women, unbridled Tory, and savage snob—showed that if most noble families contrived to conceal their

black sheep and to hide their skeletons in cupboards, there still existed aristocrats whose behavior was not only irresponsible and immoral but brazenly so. There also still existed many of those highly eccentric noblemen of whom the English aristocracy seems always to have bred a higher proportion than the aristocracies of other nations. There was, for instance, the queen's bête noire, the duke of Sutherland, whose passion it was to ride on fire engines and to drive the locomotives of the Highland Railway, to the construction of which he contributed £250,000; there was the duke of Portland, who always wore three pairs of socks with his cork-soled boots and used a handkerchief three feet square and who built an underground tunnel a mile and a half long between Welbeck Abbey and the town of Worksop so that no one would notice his occasional excursions to his London house, the garden of which was surrounded by a ground-glass and cast-iron wall eighty feet high. And there was Charles Scarisbrick, the immensely rich scion of an ancient Roman Catholic family, who commissioned that archpriest of Gothicism, Augustus Welby Pugin, to reconstruct, without too nice a regard for expense, the family seat, Scarisbrick Hall in Lancashire, where its owner thereafter lived in seclusion, declining to speak even to his steward and causing his neighbors to gossip about a *ci-devant* mistress with numerous bastard children in Germany and a gambling house in Paris.

But these aristocrats were exceptional. More characteristic of the class was the duke of Westminster, a model landlord, a keen sportsman, a generous benefactor of numerous charities, a good and faithful husband, a kind father to fifteen children, and, according to George Wyndham, a "chivalrous gentleman" and the "nicest man" he had ever met. It was such men as this that led Charles Kingsley to observe in 1862 that there was "no aristocracy in the world" that had "so honourably repented" and that had "so cheerfully asked what its duty was, that it might do it." And, certainly, for all the peccadilloes of its less penitent members, the Victorian aristocracy skillfully adapted itself to the changing conditions of its time, taking note of the European revolutions of 1848 and of the rise and eclipse of the English Chartists, discarding frivolity for seriousness, turning from Dionysus and Aphrodite to God. It was a revealing sign of the times that Lord Hatherton contended that in 1810 only two gentlemen in Staffordshire had family prayers and that in 1850 only two did not.

Thus reformed, the aristocracy was enabled to retain its power. In the 1865 House of Commons well over two hundred members were the sons of peers or baronets and a further hundred belonged to the same class, so that at least three quarters of the lower house were connected to the upper by marriage, descent, or interest.

The power of the upper classes was even more decisive in local government. There were no more than about three hundred aristocratic families owning extensive estates, but below them in the social scale were about three thousand landed gentry owning up to three thousand acres each. And of these only a very small proportion were not active in local affairs and recognized by their acknowledged inferiors as being worthy both of responsibility and respect. Most of them derived at least part of their income from some kind of manufacture or business, mine or quarry, or from the lending of their distinguished names to some commercial enterprise, as Lord Nidderdale and Sir Felix Carbury did in Trollope's *The Way We Live Now.* Yet there were many who lived entirely on their rents; and although, as the author of *The Great Landowners of Great Britain* suggested in 1883, a country squire with a clear rent roll of £4,750 from thirty-five hundred acres would

When this panoramic view of the old City, The Heart of the Empire, *was painted in 1901, there were four and a half million Londoners (just under fourteen per cent of all the people in England and Wales), and the metropolis had grown so vigorously that its boundaries were hard to define. But the dome of St. Paul's still dominated the city's skyline.*

not have much more than £1,000 a year left when all his expenses had been met, his estate agent and solicitor had been paid, his various old relations and retired servants and retainers had been provided for, that income would allow him to live in considerable comfort. With oysters at 7d. a dozen (the equivalent of fourteen cents when the English penny was worth two cents), Dover sole at 1s. 6d. the pair (thirty-six cents when the shilling was worth twenty-four cents), veal at 8d. a pound, and pheasants 3s. the brace, he would be able to provide his family and guests with excellent food, much of it, of course, from his own farm. He could buy Ceylon tea for 1s. a pound, Costa Rican coffee for 1s. 3d. a pound, eighteen gallons of bitter ale for 17s., a dozen bottles of good Beaujolais for 18s., and a dozen bottles of Moet and Chandon champagne for £3. A bottle of Dewar's Special whisky cost 3s. 6d., Canadian Club 4s., Three Diamond brandy 4s. 9d., and one hundred Excepcionales Chicas Havannah cigars 35s. 6d. He could buy himself a tweed overcoat for 25s. and his wife an elegant tea gown for 39s. 6d. or an astrakhan cape for four guineas. He would be able to employ a manservant, a coachman, a gardener, perhaps a nursemaid and a governess, and certainly at least two housemaids and a cook.

CHAPTER II

BELOWSTAIRS

At the age of sixteen, "in the year 1870," William Lanceley, one of a farmer's nine children, "left home with a carpet bag, containing an extra pair of trousers, a change of underclothing and five apples. With fivepence in his pocket he walked five miles to begin his career as foot-boy to the local squire."

On arrival, he later recorded, "I was met at the door by the footman, who, in turn, took me to the butler's room, where a most awe-inspiring individual about six feet high, portly, and dignified, told me what my duties were to be . . . first light the servants' hall fire at six o'clock a.m., clean the young ladies' boots, the butler's, house-keeper's, cook's, and ladies'-maids', often twenty pairs altogether, trim the lamps (I had thirty-five to look after), and all this had to be got through by 7.30. Then lay up the servants' hall breakfast, take it in and clear up afterwards. Tea was provided at breakfast for the women servants and beer for the men. . . . The beer was drawn from seventy-gallon casks into a leathern jack and drunk from pewter and ordinary beer horns. A fine of a penny was enforced if a man drank from a glass.

Sunday Times Magazine, LONDON

This maid's cheery smile belies the harrowing routine of her work. She was up at six in the morning and, if she was lucky, could go back to bed after sixteen straight hours of such chores as keeping the coal scuttle (above) filled.

"My day's work first followed on cleaning knives, house-keeper's room, silver, and mirrors; lay up the servants' hall dinner; take it in and wash up . . . help to carry up the luncheon; wash up in the pantry; carry up the dinner to the dining-room and, when extra people dined, wait at table; lay up the servants' hall supper; clear it out and wash up. This brought bedtime after a day's work of sixteen hours. . . . My wages were £8 a year. . . . After four years' service I was offered a holiday as the family were paying a round of visits . . . and those servants who cared to take a holiday did so. Very few did in those days and no servant would dream of asking for one unless the family were away from home. My holiday was three days. . . ."

This footboy and his female counterpart, the kitchenmaid, whose wages would usually be about £6 a year, were the lowest class of a hierarchy of indoor servants, with rules of procedure quite as strict as—and in many houses much stricter than—those governing the relationships of their masters and mistresses.

"A strange ritual took place over the midday meal in the servants' hall [at Longleat, according to the marchioness of Bath]. The under servants first trooped in and remained standing at their places until the upper servants had filed in in order of domestic status. After the first course the upper servants left in the following manner:

The occasional insufferable hauteur of servants is reflected in this Punch *cartoon. The mistress has asked her footman why he wishes to resign, and is told that "master were seen last week on the top of a homnibus, and I couldn't after that remain any longer in the family."*

When the joint, carved by the house steward, had been eaten and second helpings offered, it was ceremoniously removed by the steward's room footman who carried it out with great pomp, followed by the upper servants, who then retired to the steward's room for the remainder of their meal; while the housemaids and sewing maids scurried off with platefuls of pudding to eat in their own sitting-rooms."

In other great houses the upper servants had their meals in their own dining room, leaving the servants' hall free for their inferiors. But whatever the method of eating meals, each servant in every household was very conscious of his particular status. At the top of the scale were the house stewards and butlers, then came the valets and lady's maids, next the housekeepers ruled their regiments of housemaids and laundrymaids, the chefs and cooks their kitchenmaids, the underbutlers their footmen, and the footmen their footboys. Outside there were headcoachmen, undercoachmen, grooms, and stableboys as well as headgardeners, undergardeners, gardenboys, and odd men. The governess, with her nurses and nursemaids, ruled a quite separate department of the household.

Each servant was as careful never to touch work beneath his status or outside the limits of his prescribed sphere as any inflexible trade unionist. Richard Henry Dana, son of the Ameri-

can author, who was invited to stay at Althorp by Lord and Lady Spencer in 1875, was asked to help a fellow guest mark out the tennis court, as the odd man was busy with some other duty and neither the gardener nor the footmen would demean themselves by stooping to an odd man's work. The young duchess of Marlborough once rang the bell and asked the butler who answered the call to "set a match to an already prepared fire." He made "a dignified bow and, leaving the room, observed, 'I will send the footman, Your Grace.'"

There were certainly servants enough for these strict demarcations of responsibilities. The Dowager Lady Leigh employed thirty at Broughton Castle, though she had no more than about £4,000 a year at her disposal. The duke of Westminster had fifty indoor servants at Eaton Hall and forty gardeners besides coachmen, grooms, and stablemen. No country house of similar size was run with many fewer servants than this. In his book *The Gentleman's House*, Robert Kerr, the architect, devoted particular attention to their accommodation and the separate rooms in which their work should be done. There should, Kerr wrote, be nine divisions, including upper and lower servants' offices, kitchen, laundry, bakery and brewery offices, cellars storage, outhouses, and servants' private rooms. The upper servants' offices should include the housekeeper's room, her stillroom, storeroom, and china closet as well as the butler's room with his pantry and plate scullery. In the lower servants' offices there should be a knife room, shoe room, lamp room, and brushing room. The laundry offices were not complete without a washhouse, drying room, mangling room, ironing room, folding room, and laundrymaids' room. And the kitchen offices would require, in addition to the vast kitchen itself, a scullery, pantry, meat larder, game larder, fish larder, dairy, dairy scullery, and numerous closets, cupboards, stores, and outhouses. At Bear Wood, the house he designed for John Walter of the *Times*, Kerr put his theories into practice and produced in the rambling servants' wing a positive maze of rooms around the kitchen court and leading off the housekeeper's corridor, the men's corridor, the butler's corridor, and the transverse corridor. There were two back staircases, one for the women servants and one for the men.

The servants' sleeping accommodation at Bear Wood was not uncomfortable. But in many older houses it was atrocious. In London it was not in the least unusual to find two, three, or even four footmen sleeping in one bed in a damp, cold cellar into which daylight never penetrated. In some town houses the butler's and the house-keeper's rooms, as well as the servants' hall, were down in the cellar too. The wages paid were scarcely a compensation for such living conditions. In the 1860's an experienced house steward or a groom of the chamber could expect as much as £75 a year, £20 more than a house-keeper or a butler. A good chef would also be paid on this scale, although particularly expert chefs were paid considerably more by employers anxious to retain their services: Lord Sefton paid his chef £300 a year; and in the 1890's the royal chef, Menager, was paid £400 a year, "a magnificent salary," commented one of his apprentices, who had only £15, "and it enabled him to live extremely well. He had a London house and because of his position he did not live in the servants' quarters but came to Buckingham Palace each day by hansom cab, [wearing] an immaculate top hat and well-cut frock coat." But then M. Menager was an artist—his *rosettes de saumon au rubis* were masterpieces of world renown—and he had an enormous staff to supervise. Under his jurisdiction were eighteen chefs, eight of whom had their own tables in various parts of the palace kitchen with large staffs of their own, not to mention the pastry cooks, the roast cooks, the larder cooks, the confectionary chefs and bakers, the assistant chefs and apprentices, the kitchenmaids, the scullery maids, and the scourers. A plain cook in a less exalted household would not receive more than about £40 a year, a lady's maid about £25, a housemaid about £18, a kitchenmaid about £16, a scullery maid about £10, a teaboy and a page about £6, and a little slavey in his first

This staid, imperious staff of servants ran an upper middle-class household and observed a hierarchy more rigid than that of their masters.

year would receive perhaps no more than £2.

William Tayler, footman to Mrs. Prinsep, a rich widow of Great Cumberland Street, was paid with exceptional generosity at forty guineas a year, to which he could usually add another £15 or so in tips. But he had to work hard.

I got up at half past seven, the entry in [Tayler's diary for January 1, 1837, runs], cleaned the boys clothes [the clothes of his mistress's grandsons staying in the house during the Christmas holidays], cleaned the knives and lamps, got the parlour breakfast, lit my pantry fire, cleared breakfast away and washed it, dressed myself, went to church, came back, got parlour lunch, had my own dinner, sit by the fire and red the Penny Magazine and opened the door when any visitors came. At 4 o'clock had my tea, took the lamps and candles up into the drawing room, shut the shutters, took glass, knives, plate and settera into the dining room, layed the cloth for dinner, took the dinner up at six o'clock, waited at dinner, brought the things down again at seven, washed them up, brought down the dessert, got ready the tea, took it up at eight o'clock, brought it down at half past, washed up, had my supper at nine, took down the lamps and candles at half past ten and went to bed at eleven. All these things I have to do every day.

Being a Sunday, this was a quiet day. Wednesday that week was much more "buisy, nothing but work all day — company to dinner in the parlour and a children's party in the evening, play acting, dancing and a grand supper. . . . Did not get to bed until one o'clock and very tired." All the same the next day "got up at half past seven" as usual. "Had a great deal of work to do this morning with cleaning lamps, knives and plate. All our people dine out. They go to the old lady's marreyed daughter who lives in Belgrave Square. Went at five o'clock . . . I went with the carriage and fetched home the gentry, got to bed by twelve."

Tayler considered himself to be in a good situation with considerate employers and the opportunity of eating as well as he liked. After a breakfast of cocoa and bread rolls, for dinner he might have had roast sirloin of beef with roasted broccoli and potatoes followed by preserved damson pie. Then there would be tea with bread and butter and cake. Supper of cold mutton, say, and rice pudding was at nine o'clock. In addition he got "many little nice things" that came down

from the parlor, such as a "good blow out of egg hot," a hot drink made of beer, eggs, sugar, and nutmeg. There was also "plenty of very good table ale" kept in the house, and the servants — cook, housemaid, lady's maid, and coachman — were allowed to drink as much as they liked. They also seem to have been provided with tea, which, being very expensive then at 11s. 8d. a pound, servants were usually required to buy, though they could rarely afford to do so.

In some larger households, while beer and old ale was on tap in the servants' hall, the upper servants were provided with wine and whisky with which to drink the health of their master and mistress. But in these households the food was frequently not nearly so appetizing as it was in smaller establishments.

The preparation of the food sent to the servants' hall is often grossly inadequate [a butler wrote]. The energies of the head of the kitchen department are usually absorbed by the upstairs dinner, or if not, by belowstairs social obligations. It is a principle with most cooks that they are not engaged to cook for servants; consequently the servants' hall is left to the tender mercies of the kitchen-maid. . . . The result is that a huge, badly cooked joint is sent to the servants' table. This appears cold again and again at a succession of suppers and dinners, till someone, nauseated at its continual reappearance, chops it up and assigns the greater part to the swill-tub.

Neither in the country nor in the towns did the well-to-do experience any difficulty in securing the services of as many servants as they required. Indeed, in London, so William Tayler estimated, there were at least 1,500 servants out of work all the time. Certainly in 1851 there were 121,000 "general domestic servants" in London, far more than the population of Bradford, in fact of all but nine towns in the whole of Britain. "Servants are so plentifull that gentlefolk will only have those that are tall, upright, respectable-looking young people and must bare the very best character. . . . London and every other town is over run with servants." Tayler counted the number of servants advertising for places in one week in the *Times* alone and found 380 of them. Servants who could not afford to advertise gave their names and requirements to tradesmen, or applied at a registry office, or even left London altogether and, despairing of

With the help of a pair of wooden tongs, a servant lowers a dress onto her mistress over a complicated array of undergarments. It was a demanding, if not a terribly strenuous, duty, but the kitchen with its endless scrubbings (below) required real work.

finding employment in a country house, offered themselves to farmers at annual fairs as cooks wearing a red ribbon and carrying a kitchen utensil or as housemaids wearing a blue ribbon and brandishing a broom.

Although so many were unemployed, servants in work constituted the largest single category of laborers in Victorian England. In 1871, when nearly sixteen per cent of all employed people were in domestic service, there were 68,000 male indoor servants, 37,000 private coachmen, 1,235,000 female servants, and 251,000 women self-employed as washerwomen or charwomen or as step girls, cleaning steps at twopence or threepence a house. Ten years later more than one in every seven of the entire population of England and Wales was a servant. In London the proportion was one to fifteen, in Brighton one to eleven, and in Bath one to nine.

Most of these were housemaids whose daily routine was far more arduous than that described by the footman William Tayler. In a household with three housemaids, their day began before breakfast when the head housemaid took up the carpets in the drawing room and in the master's and mistress's sitting rooms, and sprinkled used, dried tea leaves on the floors preparatory to sweeping and dusting. Meanwhile the second housemaid would be carrying out similar operations in the dining room, the library, and the smoking room while the third dealt with the schoolroom, the entrance hall, and all the grates and coal boxes except those in the drawing room, which were the responsibility of the second. While the third was still busy with the grates, the head housemaid took hot water up to the master and mistress and any guests who might be staying in the house, and made up their bedroom fires; the second housemaid performed the same duties for the governess and the children. After breakfast the three maids began work in the bedrooms and on the stairs, cleaning, dusting, turning mattresses, making beds, changing sheets, emptying slop basins. This work occupied most of the morning and, when completed, was followed by a second procession with jugs of hot water into the various bedrooms so that the household could wash before luncheon; and while the family was assembled in the dining room, the basins were emptied and cleaned, the

23

towels folded or replaced, and the fires in the downstairs rooms were made up again. When the maids had had their own meal, it was time to go upstairs again to light the fires in the bedrooms and the drawing room. Then, having changed their cotton-print working dresses for black gowns, white aprons, and caps and, perhaps, taken tea into the drawing room, they had more hot-water carrying to do; and when the family and guests were in their bedrooms changing for dinner, the maids tidied the drawing room and the other downstairs rooms that had been occupied during the day. As the dining room door closed, once again the maids went upstairs to empty the basins and tidy the rooms. And before they went to bed, the hot-water basins had to be taken upstairs for the fourth time and the fires attended to once more.

A maid's work was made laborious not only by the great size of middle- and upper-class houses, the inconvenience of their planning, and the number of their floors, not only by the equally ample size of families, in which there were, on average, six children, and by the absence of those labor-saving devices that are now taken for granted, but also by the crowded jumble of furniture, ornaments, pictures, looking glasses, and bric-a-brac of every kind that Victorian rooms contained. "Wherever you can rest, there decorate," was the advice of John Ruskin, that champion of the Gothic revival whose influence on the decorative arts was decisive. And in eager obedience to this doctrine, the Victorians rejected the restraint and simplicity in interior ornamentation that their grandparents had admired. Soon after the appearance of Ruskin's *The Seven Lamps of Architecture*, the Great Exhibi-

tion of 1851 opened its doors upon a display of objects from all over the world—ornate, confusingly elaborate, and voluptuously inventive—and upon examples of interiors overwhelming in their richness. Pieces of furniture—solid, comfortable, and exotically decorated—multiplied in number and effusiveness; plain rose-colored, silk-lined walls were overlaid with flocked and patterned papers; back-to-back settees stood upon the thick pile of Brussels carpets. Behind the heavy outer curtains there appeared figured muslin inner curtains, which were elaborately fringed. Porcelain figures, papier-mâché boxes, and cut-glass bowls were set above the white marble fireplaces beside the French clock, the candelabra, and the gilt-framed chimney glass. On a console table stood a model of a Swiss chalet brought back from Lausanne and on a purdonium, a Benares tray purchased from a nephew on leave from the Poona Horse; the embroidered handles of bellpulls hung down beside the huge landscapes and seascapes, the prints and oleographs, the sepia photographs of dead relations, and the reproductions of the pictures of Sir Edwin Landseer. Spring-upholstered chairs and spring-upholstered sofas banished earlier, less plushy seats to the attic or the sale room.

Toward the end of the century, under the influence of the prophet of craftsmanship, William Morris, the more sophisticated Victorians sent their unfashionable "Exhibition art" to the sale room also. Morris, whose designs for wallpaper, fabrics, carpets, and furniture began a new chapter in the history of interior decoration, urged people to have nothing in their houses except those objects that they knew to be useful

The Industrial Revolution offered a few early bene-fits to servants. From left on the opposite page: an urn with "pockets for milk"; "Young & Marten's Special Mangle and Wringer"; a beer dispenser, where servants might draw part of their wages in drink. Above, an iron stove. Below, the servant class was large enough to support its own magazine.

or believed to be beautiful. And gradually they began to heed his advice.

For more than a generation, though, house-maids had worked in cluttered rooms in which coal fires deposited layers of dust upon a be-wildering array of objects that required their daily attention. And in thousands of houses no servants were kept other than maids of all work, who, badly paid, often poorly fed, and usually sleeping in cold, sparsely furnished rooms, were required to do far more than cleaning, dusting, tidying, making fires, and carrying water. They had to mend clothes and darn linen, answer calls, cook and wash up, go out shopping, and run er-rands. Their working day commonly began at five or six o'clock in the morning and was some-times not over until eleven o'clock at night, and since Saturdays and Sundays were also working days, many domestic servants were occupied in one or another of their manifold duties for eighty or more hours a week. The maids of all work whom Jane and Thomas Carlyle employed at 5 Great Cheyne Row, Chelsea, were typical of their kind.

There were two kitchens in the basement of the eight-roomed, four-storied house: one at the back, which was used as a washhouse, the other at the front, where the cooking was done on an antiquated range. In the back kitchen—a cheer-less, stone-paved room where Thomas Carlyle emptied buckets of cold water over himself as he stood in a tin bath—the maid kept her clothes. And in the front kitchen, when her day's work was done at last, she lay down to sleep, but not until the master had finished his pipe, which he liked to smoke by the dying embers of the fire, sitting up late while beyond the door in the cold back kitchen the maid waited anxiously for the sounds that heralded his departure upstairs to bed. Both kitchens were dark, and as Thea Holme has written:

... in the winter servants must have grown accustomed to working in semi-darkness. To cook a meal by the light of the fire and one candle (Jane was careful with candles, which cost tenpence a pound); to wash up without being able to see which was a stain and which the pattern on the plate; to pack away food in deep-set cupboards where it was difficult to make out what stood at the back of the shelf; to keep every corner swept clean of the stone-flagged floor, where stray

25

crumbs attracted armies of black-beetles and mice housed in the wainscot; all this must have presented problems to the conscientious servant. To clean and be clean, in perpetual twilight, by means of pump-water and kettles, required a high degree of patience, hardihood and industry.

Working in stygian gloom for a temperamental mistress, who was kind one minute and lost her temper the next, and for a selfish and demanding master, who, according to his wife, "considered [it] a sin against the Holy Ghost to set a chair or a plate two inches off the spot they have been used to stand on," must have been exasperating to the most placid and patient girls. It is scarcely surprising to learn that in their thirty-two years at Cheyne Row the Carlyles had thirty-four maids—excluding charwomen, young girls who "had never been out before," and similar make-shifts and stopgaps—particularly as their wages were no more than £8 to £12 a year, as dinner sometimes consisted of a bit of cold roast meat and supper of porridge, and as the kitchen bed, so one of them discovered, was infested with bugs. Yet, if the servants disliked working for the Carlyles, the Carlyles were equally dissatisfied with the servants. There was Jane, a clumsy, dreamy creature, who poured water over her mistress's foot instead of into the coffee pot and who became so absorbed in reading her book that she forgot to light the fire. There was a "mutinous Irish savage" with "a face like a Polar Bear" and a primitive Scottish girl, who loved answering the door but failed to announce Fanny Kemble, being "entirely in a non-plus whether she had let in 'a leddy or a gentleman,'" and who had a tiresome "follower" in the shape of a soldier, by whom she seems to have become pregnant. There was Helen, who was dirty and drank and whom her mistress discovered one day "lying on the floor, dead-drunk, spread out . . . with a chair upset beside her, and in the midst of a perfect chaos of dirty dishes and fragments of broken crockery"; "The Beauty," who spent her time looking through keyholes and reading Mrs. Carlyle's letters and who left complaining that she could not live in a house that was "such a muddle"; an "old half-dead" woman with a "shocking bad temper"; "a little girl . . . who could not cook a morsel of food or make a bed, or do any civilised thing";

another little girl who came "with a serious disease upon her, and had to be sent to hospital"; yet another who went deaf and departed complaining that she would "certainly die of grief if she went on listening to bells and never hearing them"; a "perfectly incompetent cook and servant," who "finished off by stealing eight bottles of ale"; an unbalanced creature, who capered about kissing her mistress's hands and shawl; Flo, "an incomparable small demon," who was dismissed for slander and lying; and Jessie, the last of them all, who was "only amenable to good sharp snubbing."

A generation after Jessie's departure from Cheyne Row, maidservants were still being as overworked and underpaid as ever.

I was the only servant [wrote one maid of all work in the service of a dentist at Chiswick]. I had to be up at six o'clock in the morning, and there were so many jobs lined up for me that I worked till eleven o'clock at night. The mistress explained that she was very particular; the house had to be spotless always . . . I had to clean all the house, starting at the top and working down, sweeping and scrubbing right through. Hearthstoning the steps from the front door to the pavement took me an hour alone. I was most conscientious.

The meals I remember well. For breakfast I had bread and dripping. There were often mice dirts on the dripping to be scraped off first. Dinner was herring, every day; tea was bread and marge. I didn't have a bath during the month I was there. I wasn't given the opportunity; in fact there was no time to comb my hair properly. . . .

My room was in the attic. There was a little iron bed in the corner, a wooden chair and a washstand. It was a cold, bare, utterly cheerless room. At night I used to climb the dark stairs to the gloomy top of the house, go over to my bed, put the candle on the chair, fall on my knees, say my prayers, and crawl into bed too tired to wash. Once, quite exhausted, I fell asleep whilst praying and woke in the early hours of the morning, stiff and cold, still kneeling with the candle burned down, and the wax running over the chair.

This girl's previous employer had been "a clerk of some sort" who paid her two shillings a week and appeared to have little money himself but "liked the idea of having a maid and obliged her to wear a cap, a collar, cuffs, and an apron." The same was true of Charles Dickens's parents, who, when John Dickens was employed as a clerk in the Navy Pay Office at less than £200 a year, considered themselves able to afford a maid. The Carlyles had no more than £150 a year between 1848 and 1855, and when Thomas began to earn more, they felt themselves entitled to two servants instead of one. Indeed, several authorities, including Mrs. Isabella Beeton, the author of *Beeton's Book of Household Management*, set down the number of servants that might be kept on various incomes; and it was universally agreed that a clerk in steady work could well afford the services of a maid. So it was that in those long streets of houses where, row upon row, lived the families of the Victorian lower-middle class there was scarcely a household that did not have the services of a maid, as the Pooters (see page 79) of Brickfield Terrace, Holloway, had their Sarah and the Micawbers of Windsor Terrace, City Road, had Clickett, their little orphan from St. Luke's Workhouse, who tells David Copperfield she is an "orfling."

BY COURTESY OF THE *Sunday Times Magazine*, LONDON

The age demanded this sort of clutter in a drawing room, and coal stoves demanded that many servants dust it.

CHAPTER III

THE MIDDLE CLASS

Writing in 1887, the year of the queen's Golden Jubilee, the novelist Sir Walter Besant, whose life exactly spanned the Victorian Age, considered that in any sound historical study of the times in which he was living "the great middle-class—supposed . . . to possess all the virtues; to be the backbone, stay, and prop of the country—must have a chapter to itself."

Besant himself had been born in a middle-class home in Portsmouth, the fifth of the ten children of a moderately prosperous merchant; and looking back to the days of his youth, he described how different the middle class was then from what it had since become. "In the first place it was far more a class apart," he wrote. "In no sense did it belong to society. Men in professions of any kind [except in the Army and Navy] could only belong to society by right of birth and family connections; men in trade—bankers were still accounted tradesmen—could not possibly belong to society. That is to say, if they went to live in the country they were not called upon by the county families, and in town they were not admitted by the men into their clubs, or by ladies into their houses. . . . The middle-class knew its

own place, respected itself, made its own society for itself, and cheerfully accorded to rank its reverence due. . . . Middle-class life—especially in the country—was dull, far far duller than [it is today in 1888] even in the quietest country town. The men had their business; the women had the house. Incomes ran small; a great deal was done at home, that is now done out of it. . . . All the jam was made at home; the cakes, the pies, and the puddings, by the wife and daughters; the bread was home-made; the beer was home-brewed. . . . Everybody dined in the middle of the day. Therefore, in the society of the country town dinner parties did not exist. On the other hand, there were sociable evenings, which began with a sit-down tea with muffins and tea-cakes, very delightful, and ended with a hot supper. Tobacco was not admitted in any shape except that of snuff into the better kind of middle-class house; only working men smoked vulgar pipes; the Sabbath was respected. . . . For the young there was a fair once a year."

Since then the life of the middle classes had undergone great changes as their numbers had swelled and their influence had increased. They had successfully invaded the hitherto impregnable precincts of the upper classes and, while spreading among them their own fundamental values, had taken over many upper-class manners and customs. Books of etiquette and guides

During the era the middle class grew in power and wealth until many of its members were invading the aristocracy. The family opposite could have afforded the teapot above, which came from Harrod's tonish department store.

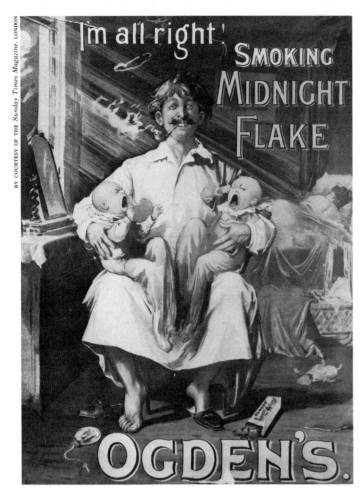

to deportment—publications with such titles as *The Habits of Good Society, Don't: A Manual of Mistakes and Improprieties more or less prevalent in Conduct and Speech,* and *Party-Giving on Every Scale*—were published in ever-growing numbers and were so widely read that many of them became best sellers in numerous editions. Eventually they imposed upon middle-class society a code of conduct that was universally recognized as being correct and that was, in fact, far more rigid than that observed by the aristocracy, whose inbred self-confidence allowed them to interpret the rules of propriety more or less as it suited them.

"Don't tuck your napkin under your chin, or spread it upon your breast," advised one influential late Victorian authority, evidently conscious of how many vulgar habits still existed among aspirants to middle-class gentility. "Don't eat from the end of the spoon, but from the side. Don't gurgle, or draw in your breath, or make other noises when eating soup. . . . Don't bite your bread. Break it off [but not] into your soup." This authority continued in another section:

Don't expectorate on the sidewalk. . . . Don't use slang. There is some slang that, according to Thackeray is gentlemanly slang, and other slang that is vulgar. If one does not know the difference, let him avoid slang altogether. . . . Don't use profane language. . . . Don't use meaningless exclamations. . . . Don't call your servants *girls.* Call the cook *cook,* and the nurse *nurse,* and the housemaids *maids.* . . . Don't conduct correspondence on postal-cards. . . . Don't sit cross-legged. Pretty nearly everybody of the male sex does—but nevertheless, don't. . . . Don't, however brief your call, wear overcoat or overshoes into the drawing room. If you are making a short call, carry your hat and cane in your hand, but never an umbrella. . . . Don't attempt to shake hands with everybody present. If host or hostess offers a hand, take it; a bow is sufficient for the rest. Don't in any case, offer to shake hands with a lady. The initiative must always come from her. By the same principle don't offer your hand to a person older than yourself, or to any one whose rank may be supposed to be higher than your own, until he has extended his.

"If . . . you meet a lady whom you know slightly, you must wait till she bows to you," another best-selling manual informed its male readers. "You

THE "SPÉCIALITÉ CORSET"

IS A DREAM OF COMFORT.

During the Victorian age advertising became a highly-organized business. As the examples on these pages suggest, almost everything was hawked in the press and on posters, often with the predictable outrageous claims.

then lift your hat quite off your head with the hand, whichever it may be which is farther from the person you meet. You lift it off your head, but that is all; you have no need, as they do in France, to show the world the inside thereof; so you immediately replace it. In making this salute you bend the body slightly. If, as should rarely occur, you happen to be smoking, you take your cigar from your mouth with the other hand."

"It is a piece of bad manners to enter the theatre late, disturbing the audience and annoying the singers," *Manners for Men* counseled those more used to cheaper seats than to private boxes. "In these boxes refreshments are frequently carried round by attendants. . . . Should they appear, it is the duty of the gentleman of the party to ask the lady or ladies if they wish for any, and to pay for what is consumed. It is, however, a rare thing for ladies to eat or drink at the play. The gentleman also pays for the programme."

Ladies in their turn were told not only that it was bad form to eat or drink at the play, but were given the most detailed instructions as to

how to comport themselves when they were permitted to eat. They were told to remove their gloves as soon as they sat down at the dinner table and to make sure they chose the correct implements to cut up their food and to convey it to the mouth:

Soup should be eaten with a table spoon, and not with a dessert. Fish should be eaten with a silver fish-knife and fork. All made dishes, such as rissoles, patties, etc., should be eaten with a fork only. In eating asparagus a knife and fork should be used. Salad should be eaten with a knife and fork. Jellies, blancmanges, iced puddings, etc., should be eaten with a fork. . . . When eating cheese, small morsels of cheese should be placed with a knife on small morsels of bread, and the two conveyed to the mouth with the thumb and finger, the piece of bread being the morsel to hold as the cheese should not be taken up in the fingers, and should not be eaten off the point of the knife. As a matter of course, young ladies do not eat cheese at dinner parties.

Every activity of the lady's day was covered by these manuals. She was told exactly how to behave in any circumstance in which she might find herself. She was given advice about her underclothes: "a virtuous woman has a repugnance to excessive luxury in her underclothing. She does not like too much lace embroidery or ribbons and bows. . . . To wear the garter below the knee is against all rules of taste . . . the night chemise should reach down to the feet and have long sleeves." She was warned against applying more face powder than would be sufficient to leave the spectator in doubt "as to whether the skin is imperceptibly veiled by a thin natural bloom." She was even told what to say when asked to dance. *Society Small Talk*, published in 1879, maintained that the phrase "I shall be very happy" had "disappeared in company." Ladies must now respond, having glanced down at their cards, "Certainly I am not engaged for number five, nine or thirteen" or "I am afraid I have not one to spare except number fourteen, a quadrille" or "I will give you a dance if you will come for it a little later, I am engaged for the next three dances."

Control over the countenance is a part of manners [enjoined *The Habits of Good Society*]. As a lady enters a drawing-room, she should look for the mistress of the house, speaking first to her. Her face should wear a smile; she should not rush in head-foremost; a graceful bearing, a light step, an elegant bend to common acquaintance, a cordial pressure, *not shaking*, of the hand extended to her, are all requisite to a lady. Let her sink gently into a chair. . . . Her feet should scarcely be shown and not crossed. . . . An elegantly-worked handkerchief is carried in the hand, but not displayed so much as at dinner parties. A lady should conquer a habit of breathing hard, or coming in very hot, or even looking very blue or shivery. Anything that detracts from the pleasures of society is in bad taste.

No aspect of middle-class life was left untouched, from the necessity of a young lady having a good chaperon—"a lady possessing a large circle of acquaintances, who is popular as well as good-natured"—to the size of visiting cards, the inscription to be printed on them, and the rules of their delivery:

A lady's card is larger than a gentleman's. The former may be glazed, the latter not. . . . A young lady does not require a separate card so long as she is living with her mother. . . . Cards should be delivered in person,

and not sent by post. A lady should desire her man-servant to inquire if the mistress of the house at which she is calling is "at home." If "not at home," she should hand him *three* cards: one of her own and two of her husband's. . . . If the answer is in the affirmative, she should, after making the call, leave *two* of her husband's cards on the hall-table, and neither put them in the card-basket nor leave them on the drawing-room table, nor offer them to her hostess, all of which would be very incorrect. When the mistress of the house has a grown-up daughter or daughters, the lady leaving cards should turn down one corner of her visiting card—the right-hand corner generally—to include the daughter . . . in the call.

Although such strict rules of behavior might well have been expected to inhibit the pleasure of living, most middle-class families contrived to derive the greatest enjoyment from life. Francis Kilvert, a young Wiltshire curate, recalled blissfully happy days walking in the English countryside beneath the white blossoms and the delicate light green leaves of the pear trees, with "larks mounting, bees humming, lambs playing, children in the lanes gathering violets and primroses . . . and a coot skimming along the surface of the lake with a loud cry and a rippling splash." He wrote in his diary of driving about the lanes in the vicar's dogcart, skating on the ice by torchlight, going to a panorama by magic lantern of Dr. Livingstone exploring Africa, gathering nuts in the woods with a party of children "amidst shouts and screams of laughter." He also wrote of being invited to a croquet party where he met a pretty girl "in a black velvet jacket and light dress, with a white feather in her hat and her bright golden hair tied up with a blue riband"; falling in love with her; approaching her father, who was "a good deal taken back," since the impoverished suitor had no more than a sovereign to call his own; drying the flowers of the nosegay she had given him and pressing them in an album; believing it impossible that he would ever forget her; meeting other girls and falling in love again with one of them, "a tall handsome girl with very dark hair, eyebrows and eyelashes and beautiful bright green eyes"; attending tea parties and church fetes, picnics and archery contests, and dances with claret cup and parsnip wine; and generally finding life "so curious and wonderful."

For the middle classes the English summer

Dickinson's Comprehensive Pictures of the Great Exhibition of 1851, 1853–1854

In the Crystal Palace, built for the Great Exhibition of 1851, visitors found exhibits of domestic articles turned out by the industrial revolution.

was, indeed, delightful. There were tennis parties—"such a pleasant way of seeing one's friends," thought the American wife of a Cambridge lecturer, who gave them cake and "thin bread and butter and tea all set out on a table in Peterhouse Garden, and Kate in her pretty cap and apron to wait on everybody." There were small, informal tea parties and large garden parties, where the guests would be entertained by a band and refreshments would be served in a marquee or at tables under the trees. "Rugs and Persian carpets are spread on the lawn upon which seats are placed so that should the grass be damp the guests need not fear taking cold," one of those invaluable guides to middle-class behavior informed the uninitiated. "The refreshments indispensable are tea and coffee, sherry

and claret cup, cake and biscuits . . . fruit and ices. . . . The quantity of claret cup drunk depends upon the number of gentlemen present, and also whether they are players of lawn-tennis, in which case there would probably be a run upon iced cups." Often there were croquet parties—"how much I enjoyed those Thursday afternoons when my friends used to come round to play croquet!" a Nottinghamshire doctor's daughter recalled.

We played on the lawn behind the house; and the dogs used to bark in great excitement and chase the balls from hoop to hoop. It was rather a sloping lawn and sometimes the balls rolled away down the bank and into the rock garden. One day the vicar's son, who was at Cambridge with my eldest brother, knocked my ball into this rock garden and he came to help me find it. We couldn't see it at first; but then we both discovered it at the same time behind some trailing aubrietia, and, stooping down to pick it up, our hands touched. We had been talking up till then;

33

but now we were silent. We stood up; and just stayed there, looking down at the ball. I know he wanted to kiss me. You couldn't be seen from the lawn in the rock garden. And then he suddenly took off his straw boater and he did kiss me on the cheek. I wanted to look up, so that he could kiss me properly; but I was too shy. I felt I was blushing dreadfully. Afterwards, when we had finished the game, we all sat under the willow tree drinking lemonade that mother had made for us. The others were all talking as usual, but I don't think I said a word. He went back to Cambridge soon after that; and then went out to India. I never saw him again. That was the first time anyone had kissed me. I was nineteen.

Most evenings were spent at home; and since inactivity was considered reprehensible, not to say immoral, all the members of the family occupied themselves in playing games or reading or in some other educational or artistic pursuit. Some would draw or paint whereas others did fancywork, rolled paper-work, or embroidery; made models in wax or pictures with shells; pressed flowers in books; painted fire screens; decorated bellpulls; or sewed dresses from the cutout paper patterns in the *Englishwoman's Domestic Magazine*. There were kaleidoscopes to play with, and stereoscopes, and zoetropes, which, when quickly revolved, made pictures of animals move and jump. There were magic lanterns and folios of prints and water colors to look at. There were all manner of games to play — card games and board games, paper and pencil games, whist and loo, piquet and Pope Joan, halma, solitaire and patience. Above all there was music.

In the houses of the richer families, professional musicians were employed to perform before the guests; but in less-privileged households the entertainment had to be provided by the members of the family and their guests themselves. No self-respecting middle-class home was without a piano; few daughters were not taught to play, though far from all played tunefully; and most fathers liked to sing. The result seems often to have been the kind of party that the wife of the Reverend Archer Clive, rector of Solihull, regretted having given one summer evening in 1846. "It was not a success," Mrs. Clive wryly admitted. "There was too much bad music tonight. A little is all very well, but tonight it was the staple. The wretched Iringhams and Edwards brought their young children, to do them good as they said, not thinking of the harm to us. The Crowthers played something wrong all through the first bar, and then got up a horrid glee for two pianoforte players, one harp and four voices, which was truly dreadful for

All of these people came from the middle class, the wellspring of some of England's most gifted men and women. Above is the Scottish missionary and explorer, David Livingstone.

Marian Evans rebelled against her strict evangelical upbringing and, under the name of George Eliot, wrote durable novels about the lives of middle-class people in her native Warwickshire.

A formidably gifted engineer, Isambard Kingdom Brunel built the Great Western Railway, as well as steamships, bridges, tunnels, and the Great Eastern, the ship that laid the Atlantic cable.

discord. I sang as badly as usual. And Archer . . . set off on the wrong note and kept steadily wrong all the way."

While young children were not often taken to musical parties, adults joined in children's games with unremitting zest. They played blindman's buff, hide-and-seek, hunt the thimble, charades, twirl the teacher, musical chairs, postman's knock, shadow buff, my lady's toilet, come-and-sit-ye-down-by-me-love, and all those other games whose rules—such as they were—have long since been forgotten. And when the company collapsed, exhausted, there was sure to be some member of the party who could keep them entertained with a conjuring trick or a comic song or by making a tortoise from muscat raisins and their stalks, carving a pig out of an apple, or constructing a set of Chinaman's fangs from an orange peel.

The excitement engendered at these evening parties frequently came close to hysteria, particularly at Christmas, when the party season was at its height. "Such dinings, such dancings, such conjurings, such blind-man's-buffings, such kissings-out of old years and kissings-in of new ones!" wrote Dickens of one happy Christmas when his children were young. He had taken them to a party given by his friend the actor William Charles Macready, and he had performed a country dance with Mrs. Macready. Then he had given a splendid conjuring performance, producing a plum pudding from an empty saucepan and heating it over a blazing fire in one of the other guests' top hats ("without damage to the lining") and transforming a box of bran into a live guinea pig. After supper they had pulled crackers, drunk champagne, made funny speeches, and then got up to dance; and John Forster, the critic, had seized Jane Carlyle round the waist and whirled her away. "Oh, for the love of heaven, let me go," she had cried out. "You are going to knock my brains out against the folding doors!" And Forster had replied, "Your *brains*! Who cares about their *brains* here? *Let them go!*"

Nearly everyone looked forward to Christmas then: to the hot roast beef and the turkey; the plum pudding, which was brought into the dining room and placed on the big mahogany table with a sprig of holly stuck on top, flaming in brandy; the huge barrel of Stilton cheese, damp with port; the snapdragon, that huge dish from which only the bravest or the most greedy dared pick the raisins out of the spurting flames; the presents from under the Christmas tree; the kissing beneath the mistletoe; the carolers with their

To Victorian audiences, the actress Ellen Terry was the epitome of beauty, charm, and vivacity. She began her career at the age of eight, and continued to act for well over half a century.

Charles Dickens's youth was marred by many of the hardships he later limned in his novels. He was the most popular writer of his day, and his powerful, satirical books helped speed social reforms.

Florence Nightingale displayed a genius for organization when she went to the Crimea in 1854 and set up efficient field hospitals that ameliorated the scourges of typhus, cholera, and dysentery.

Hyde Park, with its 363 acres, was a gathering place for all London even before it became the site of the Great Ex-

hibition. John Ritchie called his painting of fishing, punting, and dawdling A Summer's Day in Hyde Park.

lanterns singing in the snow outside; the walk to church, where, for once in the year, grown-ups pretended not to notice if the girls whispered or the boys let spiders loose across the hymnbook shelf in the family pew; the drives to parties and dances in the pony cart, with straw and hot bricks piled on the floor of the cart to keep the feet warm against the nightime chill, and hot baked potatoes held in muffs.

After Christmas or before, the whole family might go to London. And there they could go to the zoo or Madame Tussaud's waxworks; to the panorama to see Vesuvius erupting and the capture of Sebastopol; or to the gardens of the Crystal Palace at Sydenham, where there were exhibitions of painting and sculpture, tropical trees, and models of dinosaurs. Or there might be a fair on one of the commons in the suburbs where the children could see Madame Stevens, the Pig-Faced Lady, or the Fattest Woman in the World; the Boy With the Spotted Face; Miss Cockayne, the American giantess; or Toby, the learned pig who could "spell, read, cast accounts, tell the points of the sun's rising and setting, and the age of any party." There might even be visits to Cremorne, the famous pleasure-gardens in King's Road, Chelsea, where there were shooting galleries and side shows, medieval tournaments and river pageants; Cremorne, however, like many other pleasure-gardens, was becoming increasingly tawdry and disreputable.

There was almost sure to be a visit to the pantomime. And while the father took the boys to the toy shops in Holborn or the bazaar in Soho Square, the mother and elder daughters went shopping, looking through the enormous plate-glass windows of silk mercers and linen drapers and of the milliners and haberdashers in Oxford and Regent streets; inspecting the piles of exotic fruit and the jars of quail in aspic at Fortnum and Mason's in Piccadilly; browsing in Hatchard's bookshop close by; wandering through the various departments of Harrod's emporium in Brompton Road; hoping, no doubt, to find there was a sale at Mrs. Addley Bourne's, Family Draper, Jupon and Corset Manufacturer to the Court and Royal Family, who in 1866 had advertised "a thousand crinolines at half price, commencing at 5s. 11d." Finally, perhaps, the whole family would go to a photographer's studio and,

carefully posed, would sit staring at the camera amid the pungent fumes of collodion.

The daughters would hope to be married in their twenties. If they did not marry then, they would not be very likely to marry later; and if they did not marry at all, their life was likely to be unfulfilled and unsatisfactory. For it was almost universally held that a woman's proper place was in the home, and certainly there were few opportunities for middle-class women outside the home. Some became teachers or governesses. A few found work as secretaries, but not very many until the typewriter came into general use: there were only seven thousand women working in offices in 1881. A few became nurses; but there were still far more male nurses — as there were far more male shop assistants — than there were female. Even fewer were able to enter the professions, and those who did so succeeded only in the face of strong opposition and ridicule. The advent of women into the medical profession, for example, was sternly resisted by most male doctors. And long after Elizabeth Blackwell, daughter of a Bristol sugar refiner, and Elizabeth Garrett Anderson, a Suffolk merchant's daughter, had succeeded in getting admitted to the medical register, the *Lancet* continued to deride the ambitions of "certain *persons*" who had "succeeded in passing the examinations thrown open to them, and others may do the same," it was regretted. "But the common sense of the world and the good sense of the sex will no more permanently tolerate the unseemly invasion of an unsuitable province of labour than women, as a class, will ultimately shew themselves fitted for the discharge of the duties they have rashly and, as we believe, indecorously, undertaken."

Women, in fact, as T. H. Huxley observed, were brought up to be either drudges or toys beneath man or "a sort of angel above him," with few rights, little freedom, and no expectation of sharing man's privileges. "Be good, sweet maid," was the often-quoted advice of Charles Kingsley, "and let who can be clever."

In a happy marriage all would be well. But the ill-treated wife found it difficult to escape from her miserable predicament. Until the law was gradually changed in the 1870's and 1880's, a woman's possessions became those of her hus-

band as soon as she married. Divorce could be obtained only by an act of Parliament before 1857; and even after that, although a husband could divorce his wife for adultery alone, a wife had to prove that her husband was guilty of adultery combined with cruelty or desertion. If she was willing to face public examination on such indelicate matters, she found herself ostracized from many houses. When Effie Ruskin sought to divorce her husband, who had failed to consummate their marriage, she was severely criticized by many of her contemporaries, who agreed with the queen that the "mad wicked folly of Women's Rights" ought to be checked before the "poor feeble" female sex lost all "sense of womanly feeling and propriety."

The tea party was an indispensable ritual of Victorian life. The one above seems somewhat less suffocating than many; despite the elaborate dresses and the cluttered room with its wall of ornately-framed pictures, there is an air of informality and even gaiety about the proceedings.

CHAPTER IV

GROWING UP

Whenever the duke of Westminster returned home to Eaton Hall in Cheshire from his London house in Eaton Square, he was greeted with a welcoming clangor from the clock tower that soared above his broad, steeply sloping roofs. The tune that his carillon of twenty-eight bells played was "Home, Sweet Home," whose notes were as familiar throughout England as those of the national anthem. It was the favorite song not only of the duke but of thousands of other people, who sang it feelingly in music halls and who framed its words, in sampler and poker work, on their parlor walls. For the Victorians, to whom the concept of family assumed an almost mystic quality, there was, indeed, "no place like home." John Braham held it in the same reverence as he held England and beauty, Hannah More wrote of its "almost sacred joys," and Ralph Waldo Emerson considered that all the efforts of the English were "directed towards maintaining its independence and privacy." Emerson wrote, "Domesticity is the taproot which enables the nation to branch wide and high." He also said, "Nothing so much marks their manners as the concen-

tration of their household ties."

To many Victorians—perhaps to most—growing up was, however, a far from painless process, since unquestioning submission to their elders and betters was required of all children from their earliest years. "Children, obey your parents in the Lord!" was an injunction as inviolable as "Wives, obey your husbands!" So was that other often-repeated command, "Children should be seen, not heard." Yet, in fact, the children of well-to-do parents were not often even seen. Confined in a stuffy, sunless nursery wing, separate from the rest of the house, they spent most of their days in the care of governesses and nursemaids; attending lessons behind baize-covered doors in the schoolroom when they were old enough; going for walks well muffled against cold air, the boys with their pockets sewn up so that they could not put their hands in them, the girls enjoined to keep their heads up and their shoulders back and, if they did not do so, required to wear shoulder-yokes or backboards or to pin a piece of prickly holly round their necks; having their meals in the day nursery; going to bed in the night nursery long before they felt inclined to sleep. As a special treat they might be allowed down into the dining room after their parents—and those elder brothers and sisters permitted to eat there—had finished their meal, and they might be granted leave to dip their fingers into the

A hundred strict childhood duties seem to be weighing on the sober little creature opposite. She is Alice Liddell, the Alice of Alice in Wonderland, and Lewis Carroll took the picture. Above is a page from a primer she might have used.

41

On a sedate outing in the park, a nursemaid keeps a stern eye on her charges lest they daub mud on those spotless outfits.

fruit bowl or the silver bonbon dish. But normally their diet was confined to that unappetizing fare that was brought up to them on trays by unwilling footmen from the distant kitchens. Since all but the plainest food was considered quite beyond their digestion, the dishes on these trays would almost invariably contain plain boiled vegetables and milk puddings with, perhaps, a little steamed fish or boiled mutton or fowl. There would be porridge for breakfast; bread and butter, with a strictly rationed quantity of jam and cake, for tea; and, as often as not, a dose of some medicine after tea to serve as a tonic in cases of suspected anemia or as a laxative for constipation. Pills and powders, emulsions and syrups, castor oil and licorice, brimstone and treacle, senna and camomile tea, were all administered with alarming frequency, as were patent medicines such as Daffy's Elixir and Godfrey's Cordial, which contained a high proportion of laudanum and, if given in sufficiently liberal doses, could reduce the little

swallower to utter stupefaction for hours on end. The nursemaid in Charlotte Yonge's *The Daisy Chain*, who dosed her small charge to death, was as familiar a person in fact as in fiction. So were those self-employed monthly nurses, who could "be got at eighteenpence a day for working people and three-and-six for gentlefolks—night-watching being an extra charge." Their society was difficult to enjoy without becoming conscious of a smell of spirits, and their patients, if fractious, were more likely to be quieted with a spoonful or two of sugared gin than with a lullaby or a chapter of the *Water Babies*. According to a report of 1844, "a great number of children perish, either suddenly from an overdose, or, as more commonly happens, slowly, painfully and insidiously."

Augustus Hare, who achieved modest fame as a water colorist and a writer, described some other horrors of Victorian childhood. Born in 1834 in Rome, the youngest of several children of a gentleman from Sussex, he was adopted soon after his first birthday by his godmother, the widow of an uncle, who then lived at Hurstmonceux near her brother-in-law, Julius, rector of the parish. Augustus was devoted to his

42

mother and to his nurse. His uncle Julius, however, made his life a misery.

In the most literal sense, and in every other, I was "brought up at the point of the rod" [Hare recalled in his memoirs]. Uncle Julius was . . . always sent for to whip me when I was naughty! These executions generally took place with a riding-whip, and looking back dispassionately through the distance of years, I am conscious that, for a delicate child, they were a great deal too severe. I always screamed dreadfully in the anticipation of them, but bore them without a sound or a tear. . . . As an example of the severe discipline which was maintained with regard to me, I remember that one day when we went to visit the curate, a lady . . . very innocently gave me a lollypop, which I ate. This crime was discovered when we came home by the smell of peppermint, and a large dose of rhubarb and soda was at once administered with a forcing spoon, though I was in robust health at the time, to teach me to avoid such carnal indulgencies as lollypops for the future. For two years, also, I was obliged to swallow a dose of rhubarb every morning and every evening because—according to old-fashioned ideas—it was supposed to "strengthen the stomach"! I am sure it did me a great deal of harm, and had much to do with accounting for my after sickliness. Sometimes I believe the medicine itself induced fits of fretfulness; but if I cried more than usual, it was supposed to be from want of additional medicine, and the next morning senna-tea was added to the rhubarb. I remember the misery of sitting on the backstairs and having it in a teacup with milk and sugar.

Forbidden to play with children other than his cousin Marcus, "an indulged disagreeable child," whom he thoroughly disliked, Augustus spent most of his time alone, reading improving books aloud or nursing his beloved cat and waiting until it was time for dinner—"almost always roast-mutton and rice-pudding"—or for tea, which was eaten in the cold servants' hall, where, however, the servants never sat, preferring the warmth of the kitchen. Yet if Augustus's life was a misery before his uncle's marriage, it was far worse after it, as his aunt Esther tormented him unmercifully.

In order to prove that her marriage had made no difference in the sisterly and brotherly relations which existed between my mother and Uncle Julius, Aunt Esther insisted that my mother should dine at the Rectory *every* night, and as, in winter, the late return

in an open carriage was impossible, this involved our sleeping at the Rectory. . . . Once landed at the Rectory, I was generally left in a dark room till dinner at seven o'clock, for candles were never allowed in the room where I was left alone. After dinner I was never permitted to amuse myself, or to do *anything*, except occasionally to net. If I spoke, Aunt Esther would say with a satirical smile, "As if you ever *could* say anything worth hearing, as if it was ever *possible* that anyone could want to hear what you have to say." If I took up a book, I was told instantly to put it down again; it was "disrespect to my Uncle." . . . Aunt Esther resolutely set herself to subdue me thoroughly —to make me feel that any remission of misery at home, any comparative comfort, was a gift from her. But to make me feel this thoroughly, it was necessary that all pleasure and comfort in my home should first be annihilated. I was a very delicate child, and suffered absolute agonies from chillblains, which were often large open wounds on my feet. Therefore I was put to sleep in 'the Barracks'—two dismal unfurnished, uncarpeted north rooms, without fire-places, looking into a damp court-yard with a well and a howling dog. My only bed was a rough deal trestle, my only bedding a straw palliasse, with a single coarse blanket. The

Victorian children were not always dour and subdued, as the caricaturist John Leech suggests in his 1850 drawing Young Troublesome.

only other furniture in the room was a deal chair, and a washing-basin on a tripod. No one was allowed to bring me any hot water; and as the water in my room always froze with the intense cold, I had to break the ice with a brass candlestick, or, if that were taken away, with my wounded hands. If, when I came down in the morning, as was often the case, I was almost speechless from sickness and misery, it was always declared to be "temper." I was given "sauerkraut" to eat because the very smell of it made me sick. . . . Open war was declared at length between Aunt Esther and myself. I had a favourite cat called Selma, which I adored, and which followed me about wherever . . . I went. Aunt Esther saw this, and at once insisted that the cat must be given up to her. I wept over it in agonies of grief: but Aunt Esther insisted. My mother was relentless in saying that I must be taught to give up my own way and pleasures to others . . . with many tears, I took Selma in a basket to the Rectory. For some days it almost comforted me for going to the Rectory, because then I possibly saw my idolised Selma. But soon there came a day when Selma was missing: Aunt Esther had ordered her to be . . . hung!

Although many a Victorian childhood was quite as miserable as Augustus Hare's, growing up was far from being a process of unrelieved gloom. Osbert Sitwell's nursery at Scarborough was in a dark back attic of the family's high old stone-pillared house overlooking a narrow alley through which roared the bellowing winds of winter, "tearing the words from the throats of the speakers right away into the void." But he was perfectly content. His mother was kind and indulgent, allowing him to wander in and out of her room, to lie on her bed, and to play with her pincushions and jewelry. His father, who always came with his mother to say good night to him, told him marvelous stories about knights and crusaders. His brother had so little fear of their parents that at the age of four he made a habit of going up to strangers in the street saying to them, "My Mummy and Daddy would be delighted if you would lunch with them tomorrow" —an invitation that his father felt obliged to honor, being a member of Parliament and deem-

These painted tin toys were made in Germany for the English market during the 1890's. Selling for only a penny each, they were available to almost everybody.

ing it unwise to turn constituents away from his door. Other children were even more indulged than the young Sitwells, though few were like the Murray children in Anne Brontë's *Agnes Grey*, who were permitted to give their own orders to their governess and once sent a servant to her room at half past five in the morning saying that they wanted to have their lessons before breakfast that day, then deciding to stay in bed after all. Certainly it was not at all unusual for children to be allowed to ask the maids of the house to wash their dolls' clothes.

Toys were plentiful. There were dolls with china heads and with eyes that opened and shut; there were dolls that cried and dolls that could say "Papa" and "Mama"; there were dolls that had a change of beautifully worked clothes for every occasion and dolls that lived in their own elaborately furnished houses. There were wooden dolls, painted Dutch dolls, wax dolls, dolls of rag, and dolls of leather. Charlotte Yonge, the future novelist, had twenty-one dolls in all; and she was devoted to them all, particularly to her "chief doll," a present she had been given for hemming her first handkerchief. For children who did not care for dolls there were hobbyhorses and rocking horses, jigsaw puzzles and music boxes, woolly animals, castles of molded cardboard made in Germany, models of sailing ships, Noah's arks, and regiments of lead soldiers. There were all sorts of games to play indoors; and kites, battledores and shuttlecocks,

Many nurseries were gloomy, cheerless places, but occasionally attempts were made to brighten them up. The bit of folk art opposite is a wood and canvas screen, decorated with a paper collage of children and flowers.

Godliness was stressed all the time, and its handmaiden, cleanliness, was honored with the ritual of the Saturday night bath.

hoops, and tops to play with in the garden. Most children were allowed to keep a pet, a puppy or a kitten, a dormouse or a parrot; and few children were left without books. In the earlier years of the century books written specifically for young readers tended to be moralizing tracts; but by the time the novels of Charlotte Yonge and Captain Marryat had begun to entrance their numerous devotees, romance and adventure were considered acceptable weekday reading by even the strictest parent.

"I remember so well reading *Little Folks* in the shade of the elm tree by the canal at the bottom of the garden," a Birmingham builder's daughter wrote of her young days in one of the city's new suburbs. "Every now and then a gaily painted barge would go by drawn by a horse that walked dreamily along the towpath. The bargees' wifes, hanging out the washing while the children scampered about all over the boat, would sometimes wave to us. We had picnics down there; and the boys would spit out the stones from the cherry pie, competing with each other to see who could spit the farthest into the water. We used to unlace our black boots and take off our stockings and dangle our feet over the bank. When I went back to my boarding-school I used to dream of those days and long for the term to end."

Indeed, most Victorian children who went to boarding school longed for the term to end. Augustus Hare's life at school was quite as unhappy as his life at home. At the age of nine he was sent to board with the Reverend Francis Kilvert, who kept a preparatory school for the sons of gentlemen—"a set of little monsters"—who were destined for what the English call a "public school"—in American terminology, a private boarding school. When he was thirteen he went to Harrow and afterward to Oxford. This was a typical education for boys of his class, though many, after being instructed at home by a tutor or by the local clergyman, went straight to a public school, an establishment adequately described by Sydney Smith as "an endowed place of education of old standing to which the sons of gentlemen resort in considerable numbers."

Few of those who attended a preparatory school as boarders before going on to public school relished the experience. Their doses of unpalatable medicines were continued unremittingly; the incidence of their floggings was more than likely increased; and the method of education most frequently employed resembled that adopted at the "infantine Boarding-House of a very select description" run at Brighton by Mrs. Pipchin, whose system it was, as Dickens tells us in *Dombey and Son,* "not to encourage a child's mind to develop and expand itself like a young flower, but to open it by force like an oyster...."

A large proportion of school hours, both at preparatory schools and public schools, was devoted to the classics, there being, as Sir George Young observed, hundreds of people who could teach them and hardly anyone who could teach anything else. "The Greek and Latin grammars, and portions of the easier classic authors—cricket—boating—the price of tarts, and of wine by the bottle, and perhaps the names of the head and assistant masters of the school," these were, so it was alleged in 1850, "the particulars of the [public-school boy's] vast sum of knowledge."

At Rugby, as we learn from that celebrated old Rugbeian Thomas Hughes, whose account of Tom Brown's adventures there was published in 1857, "young gentlemen of all ages ... expended such part of their energies as was devoted to Latin and Greek upon a book of Livy, the Bucolics of Virgil, and the Hecuba of Euripides,

46

which were ground out in small daily portions."
Yet Tom Brown's father does not "care a straw
for Greek particles." All he wants is for his son to
"turn out a brave, helpful, truth-telling Englishman, and a gentleman, and a Christian." Tom
himself puts at the head of his list of ambitions
"to be A 1 at cricket and football and all the
other games" and to be able to stand up well
in a fight "against any fellow, lout or gentleman." He wants to get into the sixth form before
he leaves, he adds, but only so as to be able
"to carry away just as much Latin and Greek as
will take me through Oxford respectably." Most
public-school boys would have agreed with him.
When the captain of Rugby's football eleven as-
serts that he would "sooner win two School-
house matches running than get the Balliol
scholarship any day," his observation is greeted
by his younger admirers with "frantic cheers."

In the 1860's a commission, headed by Lord
Clarendon, was appointed to report on the nine
"great schools," which included Eton, Harrow,
Winchester, Westminster, and Rugby. Some
educators, called to give evidence before this
commission, severely criticized both the narrow-
ness of the schools' curricula and the amount
of time devoted to games. Surely, it was argued,
reform was badly needed in a system that required boys at Rugby, not the most classically
inclined of schools, to spend seventeen out of
twenty-two school hours in the study of Greek
and Latin and that allowed a Harrovian to spend
sixteen—or twenty if he took "every opportunity"
—hours a week playing cricket. But the headmasters—most of them clergymen—did not
agree.

"We find modern languages, geography, chro-
nology, history and everything else which a well-
educated Englishman ought to know, given up,
in order that the whole time should be devoted
to the classics," Lord Clarendon observed to the
headmaster of Eton, "and at the same time we
are told that the boys go up to Oxford not only
not proficient, but in a lamentable deficiency in
respect to the classics." The headmaster curtly
replied, "I am sorry for it." The headmasters
were not alone in their obduracy. Mr. Gladstone,
then chancellor of the Exchequer, who had been
at Eton himself, was on their side, scorning
"the low utilitarian argument in the matter of

*Children of the rich were tutored at home or
sent to school. Those less favored were taught at
village schools like this one, which was photo-
graphed in 1856.*

education, for giving it what is termed a practical
direction."

In a practical direction it certainly did not go.
There were reformers of course: following the
example of Thomas Arnold of Rugby and Samuel
Butler of Shrewsbury, such headmasters as
Cotton of Marlborough and Thring of Uppingham began to introduce modern subjects, and
even art and music, into their schedules and to
enlist the help of the senior boys in running the
school in a humane and responsible way. But
education in the majority of schools remained
severely limited while the atmosphere became
increasingly snobbish as it reflected the sharpen-
ing class distinctions in the world outside. In
those schools where free places were given in accordance with the requirements of some endow-
ment, an extremely clear division was drawn
between the poor boys and the sons of the well-
to-do, a discrimination carried so far in some
schools that the two were separated in class by
breast-high partition walls and were required to
play games at different times.

In the earlier years of the century many a
country squire had considered that the local
grammar school offered a perfectly adequate
schooling for his sons; and some country squires
still thought so, caring as little as their ancestors
had done that they and their heirs spoke in the
full, thick dialect of their region. At the same

47

time some noble families still preferred the children of the house to be educated at home by tutors. But there was a growing feeling, particularly among the prosperous middle class, that in order to grow up a gentleman a boy had to be sent away from home to endure the discomforts of and learn the lessons offered by a public school. So, as railways made it easier for boys to travel far from home, new public schools were founded at a rate that, fast as it was, was not rapid enough to meet the apparently insatiable demand.

There were far fewer boarding schools for girls, and in those that existed, the curriculum was likely to be as limited as were the few activities allowed outside the classroom. In one expensive boarding school in the 1860's the day began with an hour's scripture lesson before a breakfast of bread cubes, meagerly spread with butter, and a cup of cold coffee. The girls were not allowed to read any books other than those prescribed for their lessons, nor to write any letters that were not censored by the staff, apart from one a month to their parents or guardian. They were required to wash in cold water and were forbidden to laugh. No games were played. When the weather was fine they went for a walk "by twos and twos," the older girls leading the way under the direction of a mistress, the younger girls at the back also watched by a mistress to insure that their deportment was sedate and their conversation circumspect. In this school and similar ones no attempt was made to give the girls an education remotely comparable to that provided by the better schools for boys. At most girls' schools, indeed, even mathematics and the classics were considered unsuitable subjects for a female mind.

Demands for the reform of the education of women were, however, becoming insistent. F. D. Maurice, who was deprived of a professorship for holding unorthodox views, became the first principal of Queen's College, London, founded in the face of much criticism and some ridicule for the training of women teachers. Two of the first students at this college were Dorothea Beale, a surgeon's daughter, and Frances Mary Buss, the daughter of a painter, both of whom were to become pioneers of female education, the one as principal of Cheltenham Ladies' College and the other as headmistress of the North London Collegiate School for Ladies. By the time of Miss Buss's death in 1894 several excellent day schools for girls had been founded as well as some boarding schools, like Roedean, where girls received a wide-ranging education and were even prepared for entrance to the universities.

At the beginning of the century, "universities" meant Oxford and Cambridge, the reputation of neither of which stood very high. As late as 1852 a royal commission condemned Oxford as a place of "sensual vice, gambling . . . extravagant expenditure . . . and driving, riding and hunting." At Cambridge, where there were no more than 660 members in 1841, no lectures had been given by the professor of Greek for 150 years, and the professor of Physic was required by an Elizabethan statute to limit his discourses to an exposition of the works of Galen or Hippocrates. At neither university were scholars elected to fellowships unless they were unmarried and acknowledged members of the Church of England. Certain colleges at both Oxford and Cambridge were still granting students degrees without examination in the 1840's, and most of the examinations that were held were of the most undemanding nature. Reforms were fiercely resisted. It was not until 1871 that religious tests were finally abolished, and although most colleges allowed their fellows to marry after 1870, at King's College, Cambridge, all the fellows were required to be bachelors until 1882.

Strongly as they resisted change within their own universities, the heads of Oxford and Cambridge colleges were also anxious to prevent competition from without. The University of London was not granted a charter until 1836 and Durham not before 1837. A nondenominational college was founded at Manchester in 1851, but not until after 1880 was it combined with other colleges formed at Liverpool and Leeds to become Victoria University. By then, however, several other colleges that offered a scientific education as well as courses in the arts and that

Protesting the granting of degrees to women, Cambridge undergraduates lower a female effigy on a bicycle out of a bookseller's window.

F.A. REEVE, *Victorian and Edwardian Cambridge*, 1971

would eventually develop into universities had been opened in all the most important towns of England, Wales, and Scotland; and the student population was growing fast. By the end of the century the numbers at Cambridge had risen to over thirty-five hundred, and there were female undergraduates, too, although they were not yet allowed degrees.

Undergraduates, like pupils at public schools, were almost exclusively from the middle and upper classes. For poorer children there were no such opportunities available. There were dame schools, which had changed little since the time Samuel Johnson attended one in Lichfield kept by a widow who also had a sweet shop and which were, for the most part, considered satisfactorily run if the children were kept quiet and perhaps taught to read from the Bible, often the only book in the schoolroom. There were private day-schools and Sunday schools, factory schools and ragged schools, charity schools and county schools. There were schools that called themselves academies, in which the entire complement of children were taught in one long ink-splashed room "with three long rows of desks, and six of forms, and bristling all round with pegs for hats and slates," with "scraps of old copybooks and exercises" littering the floor, and with a strange, unwholesome smell upon the place "like mildewed corduroys, sweet apples wanting air and rotten books." And there were those notorious Yorkshire Schools, where unwanted children were boarded with "no extras and no vacations" for twenty guineas a year. In one of these, which was visited by Charles Dickens under an assumed name before he wrote *Nicho-*

A knot of children pay close attention to the boisterous goings on in a Punch and Judy *show on the beach at Ilfracombe in 1894.*

las Nickleby, a court of inquiry discovered that the children were flogged without mercy and were forced to eat food that was crawling with maggots, to sleep five in a bed infested with fleas, to suffer such privations, in fact, that ten became blind and, over a period of twenty-four years, twenty-five others, aged between seven and eighteen, were buried in the village churchyard.

Few schools were quite as bad as this, but most were as ill staffed as they were ill equipped. It was discovered, for instance, that many schools in Liverpool in 1869 were "in cellars and other filthy places" and that the teachers were not merely often dirty and sometimes drunk but almost invariably ignorant of the simplest subjects that they were employed to teach. Some of them could not read or write: a few years before, in 1851, a survey indicated that there were over seven hundred teachers in the country who could not even sign their names.

Wackford Squeers's methods of teaching at Dotheboys Hall, grotesque as Nicholas Nickleby found them, were not entirely imaginary:

"We go upon the practical method of teaching, Nickleby [Squeers told his young usher], the regular education system. C-l-e-a-n, clean, verb active, to make bright, to scour. W-i-n, win, d-e-r, der, winder, a casement. When the boy knows this out of book he goes and does it. It's the same principle as the use of globes. Where's the second boy!"

"Please, sir, he's weeding the garden," replied a small voice.

"To be sure," said Squeers, by no means disconcerted. "So he is. B-o-t, bot, t-i-n, tin, n-e-y, ney, bottiney, noun substantive, a knowledge of plants. When he has learned that bottiney means a knowledge of plants, he goes and knows 'em. That's our system, Nickleby."

Most schools were run along less haphazard lines, but their effect on the pupils was scarcely preferable. Thomas Gradgrind's school at Coketown in Dickens's *Hard Times* was one of those where ideas were frowned upon, opinions suppressed, and facts alone imparted. "Teach these boys and girls nothing but Facts," Gradgrind, founder of the school, enjoins M'Choakumchild, the master. "Facts alone are wanted in life. Plant nothing else, and root out everything else. . . ."

The fees at private day-schools such as this

On holiday at the shore, a girl in a "paddling costume" helps fill her playmate's bucket.

© *Country Life,* LONDON

were commonly less than sixpence a week; yet they were often ill attended because even this was more than many parents were able to afford.

"Schools were few," wrote a Yorkshire handloom weaver's son, who, between helping his father by winding bobbins and looking after his younger brothers and sisters while his parents worked at their looms, had little time left for homework, let alone play.

There was one kept by the postmaster—that was a good school as things went, but it was 9d. a week. Only better sort of folk sent their children there. Then there was the grammar-school, richly endowed, that taught Latin free. Anything else must be paid for. None were admitted till they could read the testament and were over six years of age. And then some influence with the Vicar was necessary to secure admission. Soon after I was six I was admitted here through the influence of grandfather. . . . I was at this school till about eight learning Latin grammar and writing. I don't remember ever being required to learn the multiplication table, or working a sum of arithmetic. . . . It was a Latin school.

Although he left school at eight to go to work in a mill, this boy was more fortunate than many in having been to school at all. For in 1851 less than half the children of school age in England had ever seen the inside of a classroom, and of those that did go to school very few remained there after the age of eleven. Henry Mayhew, the

51

journalist and sociologist, accustomed though he was to degradation and misery, was often appalled by the ignorance of the poor people he interviewed for his newspaper articles. Only about one in ten of London costermongers, so Mayhew estimated, could read, and one young costermonger who claimed to have sold his wares to the prince of Naples replied to a question as to the whereabouts of Naples:

I can't say where Naples is, but if you was to ask at Euston-square, they'll tell you the fare there and the time to go it in. It may be in France for anything I know may Naples, or in Ireland. Why don't you ask at the square. . . . I never heard of the Pope being a neighbour of the King of Naples. Do you mean living next door to him? But I don't know nothing of the King of Naples, only the prince. I don't know what the Pope is. Is he any trade? It's nothing to me when he's no customer of mine. I have nothing to say about nobody that ain't no customers.

Yes he had heer'd of God [Mayhew was informed by another denizen of the London streets, a boy of about thirteen]. Couldn't exactly recollec' when he'd heard on him, but he had most sarten-ly. Didn't know when the world was made or how anybody could do it. It must have taken a long time. It was afore his time, "or yourn either, Sir." Knew there was a book called the Bible; didn't know what it was about; didn't mind to know. . . . Had heer'd on another world; wouldn't mind if he was there hisself, if he could do better for things was often queer here. . . . Had never heer'd of France, but had heer'd of Frenchmen. . . . Didn't dislike foreigners, for he never saw none. What was they? Had heer'd of Ireland. Didn't know where it was, but it couldn't be very far, as such lots wouldn't come from there to London. Should say they walked it, aye, every bit of the way, for he'd seen them come in, all covered with dust. . . . The sun was made of fire, or it wouldn't make you feel so warm. The stars were fire, too, or they wouldn't shine. They didn't make it warm, they was too small. Didn't know any use they was of; a jolly lot higher than the gas lights some on 'em was. Was never in a church; had heer'd they worshipped God there; didn't know how it was done . . . hadn't no togs to go in, and wouldn't be let in among such swells as he'd seen coming out. . . . Thought he had heer'd of Shakespeare, but didn't know whether he was alive or dead, and didn't care. Had seen the Queen, but didn't recollec' her name just at the minute. . . .

Some children were taught to read and write by their parents; but even when parents had the time or the inclination to give lessons, they were very likely to lack the ability to do so, since at mid-century a quarter or even a third of the laboring poor were totally illiterate, except in Scotland, where schooling was of a much higher standard. And even as late as 1881, according to a census report issued in that year, about twenty per cent of the population still could not sign their names.

By then, at least, the state had assumed a limited responsibility. In 1870 an education act decreed that there should be some sort of school within reach of every English child, and in 1880 school attendance was made compulsory. Ten years later most school fees for elementary education were abolished, and the school-leaving age was gradually increased: at first to eleven, in 1899 to twelve, then at the turn of the century to fourteen.

Thousands of children, unfortunately, derived no benefit from the greater number of schools, from the free places at them, or from the longer time they were expected to attend them, since they could not be persuaded or compelled to attend school with any sort of regularity. "Children are given food in a handkerchief and live in the street, coming or not coming to school at will," a schoolmaster complained in the 1890's. "Sometimes they are lost for a week or two, living meanwhile by begging or pilfering. It is useless to speak to the parents." Of those that did go to school, a large proportion sat down at their desks too cold and too hungry to concentrate on their lessons. Many others, having been at work for part of the night, were too tired to listen to the teacher. "Of course, naturally I would be partly asleep," recalled an old man of his early school days in Hulme (near Manchester), where he had worked all night for sixpence helping a man make boiled sweets. "The teacher used to come behind me and knock me off the bench. In those days the school benches had no backs. Do you follow? You couldn't lean back. Well I used to get knocked off the bench. In fact the teacher thought it was fun by his appearance."

Homeless children roamed the streets of every city. In 1880 these boys were lucky enough to find refuge in Dr. Barnardo's orphanage.

CHAPTER V

COUNTRY LIFE

Early Victorian England was still a predominantly rural country: up till the middle of the century, despite the rapid growth of the Northern and Midland industries, more people lived in the country than in towns. In many parts of the island there were yet to be found isolated communities whose way of life had changed little in centuries and where strangers were rarely seen: there was a village in the fen country of Norfolk where there were only three surnames in the entire parish.

In less remote places even in the latter half of the century, the inhabitants' knowledge of the outside world was often as sketchy as it had been two hundred years before. Pasted on the walls of the little cottage in Oxfordshire where Flora Thompson, the writer, spent her childhood there were pictures cut from newspapers, which were changed each time the walls were whitewashed; and Flora remembered one picture in particular, a print with two rows of portraits of "Our Political Leaders," which included Mr. Gladstone, Lord Salisbury, and Lord Randolph Churchill (who must surely have been "the most handsome man in the world"). Yet these men, for

The shepherd and his flock were needed to supply the rising demands of the woolen mills. Despite much idealization, rural life was nearly as bleak and demanding as city life, and few farm cottages were as comfortable as the one above.

all she knew of the world, might have occupied a different planet: they were as strange to her as Lord Burghley would have been to Flora's Elizabethan forebears. She had no idea even of what Oxford looked like, though it was no more than nineteen miles away, as she knew from having seen the figure cut on a milestone beside the turnpike. She and her sisters often wondered what Oxford was like and asked questions about it.

One answer was that it was a "gert big town" where a man might earn as much as five and twenty shillings a week; but as he would have to pay "pretty near" half of it in house rent and have nowhere to keep a pig or to grow many vegetables, he'd be a fool to go there.

One girl who had actually been there on a visit said you could buy a long stick of pink-and-white rock [candy] for a penny and that one of her aunt's young gentlemen lodgers had given her a whole shilling for cleaning his shoes. Their mother said it was called a city because a bishop lived there, and that a big fair was held there once a year, and that was all she seemed to know about it. . . . So, for some time, Oxford remained to them a dim blur of bishops (they had seen a picture of one with big white sleeves sitting in a high-backed chair) and swings and shows and coconut shies (for they knew what a fair was like) and little girls sucking pink-and-white rock and polishing shoes. To imagine a place without pigsties and vegetable gardens was more difficult. With no bacon or cabbage, what could people have to eat?

In many country communities the squires were

as little changed by the passing generations as were their tenants. In *Mr. Sponge's Sporting Tour,* which was published in 1853, R. S. Surtees described a local squire who might well have stepped out of the pages of Henry Fielding. Yet England still had hundreds of landowners very much like Lord Scamperdale. He was "a coarse, broad, large-built sort of man" with clothes to correspond, who, as far as he could manage it, did not spend "a halfpenny upon anything but hunting." He was "stumpy and clumsy and ugly, with as little to say for himself as could well be conceived . . . a square, bull-headed looking man, with hard, dry, round, matter-of-fact features that never looked young and yet somehow never got old." He lived in a fine stone Italian-style house, Woodmansterne, which, surrounded by an undulating park of eight hundred acres, had been built at immense cost by his grandfather, who had pulled down the original brick Elizabethan mansion. But, wishing to preserve the equally fine contents in good condition "against he got married," he had the house "put away in brown holland, the carpets rolled up, the pictures covered, the statues shrouded in muslin, the cabinets of curiosities locked, the plate secured, the china closeted." And he lived in a small sitting room, whose bookshelves contained, in addition to only two books, a great quantity of old spurs, knots of whipcord, piles of halfpennies, lucifer-match boxes, gun charges, hunting horns, and similar miscellaneous articles, mainly of a sporting character.

To Scamperdale, as to many another Victorian squire, hunting was a way of life. He spent £2,000 a year on it, as much as the total income of some four hundred agricultural laborers who worked on the surrounding farms. Others, particularly those who were Masters of Foxhounds in a more fashionable hunt, such as the Quorn or the Fernie, spent far more; yet there were always scores of men as eager to take over Masterships as was that indomitable and fearless huntsman Thomas Assheton Smith, squire of Tedworth in Hampshire and "certainly the best man that ever came into Leicestershire," who was still hunting four times a week in his eightieth year, who put his head in a bucket of water if he did not feel well enough to ride of a morning, and who, after a morning's hunting at Tedworth, would drive up to Westminster to vote in the Commons as member of Parliament for Andover and be back in Hampshire for an afternoon's hunting the next day. Assheton Smith would wholeheartedly have endorsed the sentiments of John Jorrocks, the cheerful, vulgar, rich London grocer of R. S. Surtees's novels, who is both astonished and delighted to become Master of the impoverished hunt of Handley Cross: "'Unting is all that's worth living for. All time is lost wot is not spent in 'unting."

There were many countrymen who felt the same about shooting, and they were prepared to talk for hours on end about game and gamekeeping and about the disgraceful depredations of poachers and, like General William Dyott, the diarist, to lament endlessly the relaxation of the game laws, which had "done more to encourage vice amongst the lower orders" than could easily be imagined.

"Then that never ending theme of poaching came up," wrote a young American girl in a letter home from her uncle's estate in Shropshire in 1851.

I cannot imagine what [an English country gentleman] would do were there no poachers. . . . He enlarges upon the villainy of poachers, upon the ingratitude of poachers, tells anecdotes about poachers, until you grow so nervous that you expect to see a poacher start up and seize the bird upon your plate. Naturally the conversation turns upon the day's sport, and you hear how that bird was winged: how another was tailered: how many cock pheasants were shot: how many hen pheasants were deprived of life: how many woodcock were put up: how many partridges flew out of one cover; how many rabbits were killed; who shot well; who shot badly; who missed fire; whose cock pheasant fell with his tail up; whose hen pheasant with her tail down; who shot on this side of the dingle, who on the other, and so forth, and so forth, and so on. Then the meet of the previous day takes its turn—who fell in leaping over this hurdle, who in taking that hedge, who fell on his feet, who on his head, where the fox was found, and where killed, and how the sport was spoiled on account of the frost, and how cold it was, and how cold it is, and how cold it is going to be, and how unusual it is, such weather unheard of at this season, and how fine the autumn has been—and then you rise from the table and you leave the gentlemen to discuss, more at large, poaching, shooting, hunting and the cold, unrestrained by female society.

In another letter this American girl described how she spent her days in the country: she would get up early, at half past seven, so as to be ready for family prayers at half past eight; after breakfast the children of the family went to the schoolroom while she and her aunt wrote letters or did some sewing before going out for a drive. Dinner was at six, and after dinner there was "a cheerful party by the drawing-room fire, reading, or sewing or playing games with the children." She would not, however, see much of her uncle during the day, for he was so often out shooting, either by himself or with his friends.

So were many other members of his class and of the aristocracy. "Marlborough and the other guns were always shooting," his duchess recalled, "for there were pheasants, rabbits, duck, woodcock and snipe to be killed. I remember a record shoot one autumn when seven thousand rabbits were bagged by five of the best English shots in one day. They had two loaders and three guns each, and every one of them had a violent headache on reaching home." The fashion at that time was for grand battues, in which the slaughter was enormous: the season's bag of pheasants at Eaton Hall in the 1890's was between five thousand and six thousand, and on the prince of Wales's estate at Sandringham thirteen hundred partridges were once shot in a single day. Lord Ernest Hamilton recorded that on an occasion when he was asked if he would "care to come out and see if we can pick up a pheasant or two," a thousand pheasants were shot in two hours.

Maintaining a big shoot was an extremely expensive business, and although about three thousand gamekeepers were employed in the country, the grand battue was a sport for the very rich. The less wealthy squire had to be content with more modest expeditions. So did the parson, if he went out shooting at all. Indeed, the sport-

In the spring, sheep, with their winter's growth of wool, had to be washed before shearing. Here shepherds put their unprotesting beasts through the process on the Yorkshire moors.

ing parson was becoming a figure of the past. There were still several clergymen who were also landowners and even a few, like Thomas Sweet-Escott, a Somerset rector, who passed on to their ordained sons both their manor houses and their livings. There were also one or two extremely profitable bishoprics, like that of Durham, which was worth—as was the archbishopric of Canterbury—£19,000 a year; and there were more than a hundred benefices in the Church of England worth over £2,000 a year. There were a good many more as valuable as the living of Framley, which in Trollope's *Framley Parsonage* brings to the incumbent an income of £900 and is offered to Mark Robarts by Lady Lufton of Framley Court in the hope that he will prove a good influence on her son, with whom he has been at Harrow and at Oxford. But the majority of Anglican clergymen, not so well connected, had less than £400 a year and a few had no more than £50. Yet, despite the relative poverty of most of them, there remained an unbridgeable social gap between them and all but a few of their parishioners.

In Flora Thompson's *Lark Rise:*

the Rector visited each cottage in turn, working his way conscientiously round the hamlet from door to door . . . when he tapped . . . at a cottage door there would come a sound of scuffling within, as unseemly objects were hustled out of sight, for the whisper would have gone round that he had been seen getting over the stile and his knock would have been recognized. The women received him with respectful tolerance. A chair was dusted with an apron and the doing of housework or cooking was suspended while his hostess, seated uncomfortably on the edge of one of her own chairs, waited for him to open the conversation. When the weather had been discussed, the health of the inmates and absent children inquired about, and the progress of the pig and the prospect of the allotment crops, there came an awkward pause, during which both racked their brains to find something to talk about. There was nothing. The Rector never mentioned religion. That was looked upon in the parish as one of his chief virtues, but it limited the possible topics of conversation. Apart from his autocratic ideas, he was a kindly man, and he had come to pay a friendly call, hoping, no doubt, to get to know and to understand his parishioners better. But the gulf between them was too wide; neither he nor his hostess could bridge it. The kindly inquiries made and an-

swered, they had nothing more to say to each other, and, after much "ah-ing" and "er-ing," he would rise from his seat, and be shown out with alacrity.

It was the same with his daughter, who visited his parishioners with equal assiduity:

considering her many kindnesses to the women, she might have been expected to be more popular than she was. None of them welcomed her visits. . . . Perhaps at the root of their unease in her presence was the subconscious feeling of contrast between her lot and theirs. Her neat little figure, well corseted in; her clear, high-pitched voice, good clothes, and faint scent of lily-of-the-valley perfume put them, in their workaday garb and all blowsed from their cooking or water-fetching, at a disadvantage.

There was just as wide a gulf between the country doctor and the rich landowner as there was between the country parson and his parishioners. The doctor might not have been treated with the hauteur with which, at the beginning of the century, her physician was treated by Lady Carlisle, who, considering it beneath her dignity even to address him directly, instructed her maid to "inform the doctor that he may bleed the countess of Carlisle." Yet the country doctor, as the novelist Mrs. Gaskell indicated in *Wives and Daughters,* would not normally presume to consider his daughter a suitable match for the squire's son; and if he were to be called in to attend a member of the aristocracy, he would not expect to be asked to stay to dinner, as would the fashionable London doctor, whose advice was sought in most cases of graver illness and whose professional prestige arrogated to itself a certain social prestige.

As the squire stood higher in the social hierarchy than the doctor, so the doctor stood higher than the farmer. The naturalist and novelist Richard Jefferies, himself a Wiltshire farmer's son, described how a farmer's daughter, who had been to a smart boarding school, reacted to the prospect of marriage on returning home to her country town after her last term:

A banker's clerk at least—nothing could be thought of under a clerk in the local banks; of course, his salary was not high; but then his "position." The retail grocers and bakers and such people were quite beneath one's notice—low, common persons. The "professional" tradesmen [pharmacists, perhaps] were decidedly better, and could be tolerated. The solicitors,

The long linen smock was traditional country garb for the lower classes. The squirely figure at right is the falconer Major C. Hawkins Fisher.

bank managers, one or two brewers (wholesale — nothing retail), large corn factors or coal merchants, who kept a carriage of some kind — these formed the select society under . . . the clergy and gentry.

Not many farmer's daughters would have aimed as high as this: it was her boarding school that gave this one her pretentious ideas. Most farmers, indeed, had no social ambitions whatsoever, even those who rented large farms, lived in comfortable, well-staffed houses, and were far better off than the parson, whom they tended to avoid, and sometimes no less well off than the local squire, with whom they would discuss common interests in the hunting field but with whom they would otherwise have no social intercourse. "If the farming men mix with the landowners in the field sports," an observer of social mores wrote in 1851, "it is upon a footing of understood inferiority, and the association exists only out of doors, or in the public room of an inn after a cattle-show or an election. The difference in manners of the two classes does not admit of anything like social and family intercourse." Nor did most farmers presume to interfere much in the running of local affairs or to have political views at variance with their landlords.

Gabriel Oak in Thomas Hardy's *Far From the Madding Crowd* is typical of his kind. A deliberate, slow, steady man, large in frame but modest by nature, formerly a shepherd, "he had been enabled by sustained efforts of industry and

A photographer provides a moment of diversion for the children on a quiet street in Cornwall. The street leads

down to a ferry, on which one could cross to the town of Fowey, whose houses are visible on the opposite shore.

chronic good spirits" to lease a farm. When he smiled,

the corners of his mouth spread till they were within an unimportant distance of his ears, his eyes were reduced to chinks, and diverging wrinkles appeared round them. . . . He wore a low-crowned felt hat, spread out at the base by tight jamming upon the head for security in high winds, and a coat like Dr. Johnson's; his lower extremities being encased in ordinary leather leggings and boots emphatically large, affording to each foot a roomy apartment so constructed that any wearer might stand in a river all day long and know nothing of damp. . . . Mr. Oak carried about him, by way of watch, what may be called a small silver clock. . . . This instrument being several years older than his grandfather, had the peculiarity of going either too fast or not at all.

On Sundays Farmer Oak went to church and smothered a yawn during the sermon; at night he went to sleep "in about the time a person unaccustomed to bodily labour would have decided upon which side to lie." He rose early to

Tea with the parson was an immutable part of country life. Here the rector of Waltham passes an hour with a member of his congregation.

tend to his animals with the utmost conscientiousness.

Farmers like Oak preferred, in fact, to concentrate on their farming, and it was generally agreed by foreign experts that they looked after both their land and animals very well. "English farming taken as a whole is at this day the first in the world," wrote a French agriculturist in 1854, "and it is about to become even better." In addition to "plenty of grass," there were "two roots—the potato and the turnip; two spring cereals—barley and oats; and a winter one—wheat; all these plants linked together by an alternating course of cereals or white crops, with forage or green crops beginning with roots or plants which require to be hoed, and ending with wheat: this is the whole secret. The English have discarded all other crops, such as sugar-beet, tobacco, oleaginous plants and [except in Kent] fruit."

What they did grow was plentiful and of excellent quality. At the same time breeds were sound and strong, and horses, rather than oxen, pulled nearly every plow. Farms were far bigger than they were on the Continent, the average

covering over one hundred acres and half the country's farm land being in holdings of about two hundred acres, though there were more than one hundred thousand farmers who had less than fifty acres each.

These smaller farmers had to work quite as hard as the laborers employed by their more prosperous neighbors; yet, for the most part, they viewed with suspicion the advent of farm machinery, especially the steam plow, preferring the hand tools that their fathers and grandfathers had used before them.

There was little farm machinery used in those days. One Staffordshire laborer recalled of the 1870's:

"Hardwork is best work," my master used to say, and did not like even to have a horse in the field. Corn was cut with a short "badging" hook and hay was cut with the scythe. A man could cut an acre of corn a day and bind it into sheaves, but usually the farmers banded themselves together and worked in groups of from twelve to twenty. Each man had a distance of so many yards to cut, known as a "natch." He would take hold of the corn stalks and hold them with his left hand and sever them near the base, holding them until he had collected enough to make half a sheaf, which would be laid at the end of the "natch"; by the time he had worked his way back again he had cut enough to finish the sheaf. . . . Men would follow one behind the other, sometimes twenty in a line; they would soon clear a field. . . . How country folk laughed when the first machines appeared. . . . Little artificial manure was used. Cow's water was collected in tanks and carted out to the fields in barrels, where it was spread with a long-handled ladle. Contractors used to collect night-soil from the towns and sell it to the farmers. . . . Women earned 1s. 6d. a day by following the horses grazing in the pastures and breaking up the dung with a long fork.

A wage of 1s. 6d. a day for men would have been good in the early 1850's, when wages in some areas were as low as 6s. a week, which, even so, the laborers were thankful to get, as they were hired by the year and could never feel secure. Often a farmer's five or six hired laborers would all live together in a single cottage with an elderly woman to look after them and cook their food. The cottage would rarely have running water or any form of sanitation; slates would be blown off the roof and never replaced; ill-fitting doors and windows would let in the wind and rain. Some cottages were mere hovels with lean-to roofs, and as late as 1885 a witness reported to a royal commission that in Somerset he had seen eleven children all living with their parents in one of these hovels and that there were many others like it.

Conditions were not so bad as this in less remote parts of the country, but overcrowding was endemic:

Some of the cottages [in Flora Thompson's Lark Rise] had two bedrooms, others only one, in which case it had to be divided by a screen or curtain to accommodate parents and children. Often the big boys of a family slept downstairs, or were put out to sleep in the second bedroom of an elderly couple whose own children were out in the world. Except at holiday times there were no big girls to provide for, as they were all out in service. Still, it was often a tight fit, for children swarmed, eight, ten, or even more in some families, and . . . beds and shakedowns were often so closely packed that the inmates had to climb over one bed to get into another. . . . In nearly all the cottages there was but one room downstairs, many of these were poor and bare, with only a table and a few chairs and stools for furniture and a super-annuated potato sack thrown down by way of hearth-rug. . . . [In some downstairs rooms, however, there were] dressers of crockery, cushioned chairs, pictures on the walls and brightly coloured hand-made rag rugs on the floor. In these there would be pots of geraniums, fushias, and old-fashioned sweet-smelling musk on the window-sills. In the older cottages there were grandfathers' clocks, gate-leg tables, and rows of pewter, relics of a time when life was easier for country folk.

It was not easy in the middle and later years of the nineteenth century. The laborer "comes home weary from his out-of-door work," one recorder of Victorian country life observed, "having eaten his dinner under hedge or tree . . . then turns into a rude bed, standing perhaps on the farther side of his only room, and out again, before daylight if it be winter. . . . He is as simple, as ignorant and as laborious as the wagon-horses that he drives. From his childhood he had learned nothing but his work and had grown up into a tall, long, smock-frocked, straw-hatted, ankle-booted fellow with a gait as graceful as one of his own plough-bullocks." He never saw a newspaper, and if he had, he would not have been able to read it. He thought of little but food.

Some laborers, particularly those who had worked in the north, remembered being contented and well-fed with "any amount of bread and bacon, and plenty of home-brewed beer, and in the winter a sure, drowsy place by the kitchen fire . . . the open hearth with its chimney corner, the fire-shine glowing out dim and ruddy upon flitches of bacon hung around the room, and reddening upon the faces of sleepy boys." But most recalled less happy times:

When I was ten I left school to work on a farm for £3 a year and my keep. . . . As a carter's lad I helped to drive the horses and when there were two I had to walk between them while leading and often got trodden on. . . . Before bridges were built we often had difficulty in getting our horses and wagons across flooded streams. Often my clothes were quite wet when I took them off at night and still wet when I put them on again next morning. On Sundays I walked ten miles home to have dinner with my parents, and then walked ten miles back to start milking. . . . I was always hungry in that place.

The usual fare for a country worker was potatoes, turnips, and cabbages with an occasional piece of bacon, slice of apple or rhubarb pie, dumpling, or oatmeal cake. At threepence a quart, milk was beyond the reach of the poorer families; but in most cottages there were jars of wine made from cowslips, elderberries, or damsons, and sometimes there might have been a pot of tea made from used leaves collected from a nearby inn.

Farm workers' wages began to improve slightly in the 1860's, when the average weekly wage of the 880,000 men over twenty working on the land rose to about fourteen shillings a week. But then a series of wet summers—followed by outbreaks of rinderpest, liver rot in sheep, and foot-and-mouth disease and accompanied by the importation of huge quantities of wheat from America, of frozen meat from South America and Australia, and of live cattle from the Continent— brought thousands of British farmers to bankruptcy. Over a million people emigrated, and scores of thousands of others left the country to seek work in the towns.

A Cornish family in the Scilly Isles earns its livelihood by preparing bunches of flowers. The bouquets will be packed in crates and shipped across to the mainland for sale.

CHAPTER VI

WORKERS

"My husband's money was only thirteen shillings a week," wrote a farm laborer's wife of her family's life in Essex in the 1870's, "and of that two shillings went for rent, leaving eleven shillings with three little children to keep. So he asked for a rise . . . but the master soon told him if he were not satisfied, he had better take a month's notice and go. . . . Well, when our notice was up, we could not get a house anywhere that we could afford, so we parted with a few things and packed the others up . . . and Will, my husband, went to London to find work. He made his way for the Edgware Road, to a young man who had been groom at the same farm that we had left. He was at a hotel, and told Will of different places to go for work. The first night he spent in London, he slept in a manger and the rats ate part of his food which he had in his pocket while he slept. The next day he got lodgings near Paddington Green . . . and he got work as horse-keeper for a railway company, and I came to London a fortnight later . . . and [found work in a shop in Westbourne Grove making straw hats]. I was in the workroom part of the time, and had my work at home the other part."

WAYLAND PICTURE LIBRARY

Unskilled laborers, like the woman opposite, earned a few shillings a week. Many lived in far worse conditions than these; there were, for instance, few lives more wretched than those of the women who worked the coal pits (above).

Every year, even before the depression of British farming in the 1870's, tens of thousands of men and women like these left the country for the towns, which, by 1851, for the first time contained more people than the country and, by 1881, over twice as many. Most of the new townspeople did not find it easy to settle: the Essex farm worker's wife, who "would have given anything to have gone back to the country," remembered crying most of the time, for her husband was on night work and she was among strangers in a city the sheer size of which was intimidating. London's population then was rapidly approaching four million. It was the largest city in the Western world; but ten years later there were four other British towns—Glasgow, Birmingham, Liverpool, and Manchester—with populations of nearly half a million, and over twenty with more than one hundred thousand inhabitants.

The smoky, foreboding aspect of many of these towns, whose buildings were often coated in dust and soot, added to the country people's misery. "I drew near the town and the tall chimneys of the factories became visible through the dense clouds of smoke," a former factory worker wrote of Leeds, a fast-growing town whose population rose to 170,000 within a few years. It exhibited

the many marks by which a manufacturing town may always be known . . . the wretched, stunted, decrepit, and, frequently, the mutilated appearance of the

67

The life of the poor was ruled by the factories, and families lived in squalid row houses that ringed them. This city is Leeds in 1885.

broken-down labourers, who are generally to be seen in the dirty, disagreeable streets; the swarms of meanly-clad women and children, and the dingy, smoky, wretched-looking dwellings of the poor. . . . We see, on the one hand, a few individuals who have accumulated great wealth by means of the factory system; and, on the other hand, hundreds of thousands of human beings huddled together in attics and cellars, or crawling over the earth as if they did not belong to it.

For the sake of cheapness, thousands of cottages were built back-to-back with privies in front and ashpits in the street, with a cellar for coal and food, and with one small room, as a Unitarian missionary wrote, "to do all the cooking, washing and the necessary work of a family in, and another of the same size for all to sleep in." Even worse than these were those dwellings built around dark, airless, noisome courts whose occupants were obliged to share a privy and a tap. The overcrowding in such courts was appalling. As late as 1881 almost a quarter of Glasgow's population of 587,000 people were liv-

ing in one room per family and almost half had no more than two; in some rooms as many as twenty people lived together, sleeping on straw. In Leeds, according to a surgeon, uncounted numbers of Irish immigrants slept in "damp cellars," one of which he described as being "without the slightest drainage, every drop of wet and every morsel of dirt and filth having to be carried up into the street; two corded frames for beds, overlaid with sacks for five persons; scarcely anything in the room else to sit on but a stool, or a few bricks, in many places absolutely wet; a pig in the corner also; and in a street where filth of all kinds had accumulated."

London was as bad as anywhere, and in many quarters worse. Hippolyte Adolphe Taine described "one of the poor neighbourhoods" down by the river, where "low houses, poor streets of brick under red-tiled roofs cross each other in every direction." He wrote, "It is in these localities that families have been discovered with no other bed than a heap of soot; they had slept there during several months. . . . One observes the narrow lodging, sometimes the single room, wherein they are all huddled in the foul air. The houses are most frequently one-storied, low,

narrow—a den in which to sleep and die. What a place of residence in winter, when, during the weeks of continuous rain and fog, the windows are shut!"

Some had no home at all but slept in the open or in hallways of buildings in London. This was the nightly experience of the mud larks, those pathetic creatures who scavenged on the river front at low tide, poking about in the mud for bits of coal or copper nails, fragments of rope, old iron and bones, considering themselves lucky if they could sell all that they had found in a day for a halfpenny, which was not enough to pay for food much less for a bed to sleep in. They could be seen among the barges at the various wharves, barefoot, stooping to peer down into the mud, their torn rags stiff as boards. They were decrepit old men and women, bent almost double with age and infirmity, and crowds of little boys and girls, some no more than six years old. None of them talked to one another but filled old hats or leaking tin kettles with the products of their search and hurried away to the rag and bottle shops to sell whatever they had found, leaving a trail of slush behind them, hoping to get enough to buy a few big crusts of bread,

but often lying down to sleep under the arches cold and hungry, longing for the day when they would find a saw or a hammer that they might sell to a seaman for a piece of meat and a biscuit.

Overcrowding in squalid, unhealthy conditions remained the lot of millions of poor families throughout the nineteenth century. There were, of course, rows of decent cottages to be found in every county: there were industrialists such as Sir Titus Salt, the Bradford manufacturer, who built a whole town—complete with eight hundred solid, well-drained houses—around his vast mill by the banks of the river Aire in Yorkshire; there were philanthropists such as George Peabody, an American merchant living in London, who put up blocks of model dwellings, which were said to have "done wonders for the health and comfort of the residents." Yet the general run of working-class housing, even after the improvement in the standards of new building in the 1870's, was, as a report stated toward the end of the queen's reign, "mean, cramped, and unhealthy."

In the 1880's Charles Booth, the Liverpool shipowner who tried to discover the causes of poverty, described areas in London where few

The washerwoman at left probably shared one small room with her children. Others like her cram a narrow alley outside their homes, opposite. One observer wrote that the effect of such conditions on the life span "is the same as if twenty or thirty thousand of these people were annually taken out of their wretched dwellings and put to death."

families occupied more than one room.

In little rooms no more than 8 ft. square, would be found living father, mother and several children. . . . Fifteen rooms out of twenty were filthy to the last degree, and the furniture in none of these would be worth 20s., in some cases not 5s. Not a room would be free from vermin, and in many life at night was unbearable. Several occupants have said that in hot weather they don't go to bed, but sit in their clothes in the least infested part of the room. What good is it, they said, to go to bed when you can't get a wink of sleep for bugs and fleas? . . . The passage from the street to the back-door would be scarcely ever swept, to say nothing of being scrubbed. Most of the doors stood open all night as well as all day, and the passage and stairs gave shelter to many who were altogether homeless. . . . The houses looked ready to fall, many of them being out of the perpendicular. . . . Most appear poverty-stricken and all have a grimy look.

Drink, as Booth and the other investigators found, was an intractable problem in many poor families. Temperance workers calculated that in the middle of the century more was spent by the working class on drink than on rent, the average drinking man, whose rent might have been five shillings a week, spending six shillings on liquor,

more than he was willing to spend on clothes and heating for his family and not much less than he gave to his wife to buy food.

Alcoholism was aggravated by the great number of establishments selling liquor and by the equally great number of illicit stills. In Manchester, for instance, there were nearly one thousand beer houses and gin shops. In Glasgow, where thirty thousand people were said to get drunk regularly every Saturday night, there was one public house to every dwelling house. Until prohibited by law, it was a common practice in many unskilled trades for employers to pay wages in public houses in whose profits they had an interest. Even in skilled trades a man who did not drink was often looked upon as an outsider, if not as downright contemptible; and there were numerous occasions when it was traditional for a worker to "stand treat" to all his colleagues.

The men were expected to do their drinking away from their place of work, but "sometimes the men would drink on the premises," a man recalled of his days in a pottery works,

and the drink was got by the most stealthy and ingenious methods, so as to elude the observation of the

Young children in a Derbyshire textile mill worked sixteen hours a day and six days a week for a weekly wage of half a crown.

overlookers. . . . The drink was got by the top gate, and women and boys were used to get drink in vessels which would have deceived a detective. . . . Then the young women were persuaded to join in the indulgence. Drink was forced upon them in many instances, if new to the business. Before night came some of these women were drunk, and didn't know where they were. Then the most lustful and villainous of the men —young men, generally—would scheme to stay all night. . . . Men were seen still stupefied with drink [the next morning]. . . . No food was wanted, and little work was done. Some of the men stole away to the beer-house, to get revived.

After such carousals the men were frequently driven to the pawnbroker, whose shop could usually be found not too far from any large public house. In 1844 there were as many as sixty pawnshops in Manchester, to which workers were obliged to cart their possessions, mostly clothes, on a Monday, hoping that by pay day on Saturday they would be able to redeem them and to pay the interest on the money they had borrowed.

In the upper working-classes, categorized by Booth as "higher class labour . . . men of very good character and much intelligence," such

practices were scorned. These artisans—compositors, watchmakers, masons, woodworkers, skilled workers in engineering firms—considered themselves as far above the ordinary worker as the bank clerk considered himself above the skilled artisan. They lived comfortably, owned their houses, perhaps, and almost certainly saved money and paid insurance premiums. Some of them earned as much as £2 10s. a week. In Birmingham public houses there were separate doors for the highly paid button makers. Artisans like this, however, formed a very small proportion of the working class in English industrial cities.

Charles Booth gave an example of one London family's budget, which he said was "typical of a great many others." The father was a casual dock laborer, aged thirty-eight; the mother was consumptive and could not work; and the son, eighteen years old, earned regular wages of 8s. a week as a carman's boy. There were two girls, aged eight and six. Their house had four rooms, but two were let. Both father and son had their dinner away from home and for this purpose the son took 2d. a day. The clergy of the neighborhood sent soup two or three times a week, but "practically no meat" was ever bought. "Beyond the dinners out, and the soup at home," Booth wrote, "the food consists principally of bread, margarine, tea and sugar. . . . No rice is used nor any oatmeal; there is no sign of any but the most primitive cookery, but there is every sign of unshrinking economy; there are no superfluities. . . . In the kitchen the son will sleep, his parents and sisters occupying the front room. Neither [room exceeds] ten ft. square; both . . . are patterns of tidiness and cleanliness. . . . This accomodation costs about 17s a month." On heating this family spent about 9s. a month, "as much as, and more than, many with double the means; but warmth may make up for lack of food, and invalids depend on it for their lives." Booth reckoned that no more than 1d. per meal per person was spent in this household ("counting the two little girls as one person") and that the expenditure was chiefly upon cheap bread, cheap butter, cheap tea, and cheap sugar.

In cases of extreme distress, men were often able to look for relief to a sympathetic employer. There were enough employers such as those

Lying in ranks of coffinlike bunks, hapless Londoners settle down for the night in a poorhouse called the Field Lane Refuge.

described by an old Staffordshire potter, who were "rarely seen at the works" or else "used to come about ten o'clock in the morning in a carriage and pair, and stay half-an-hour or an hour." Yet there were many others who, in return for an orderly, well-behaved, and contented work force, were prepared to pay good wages, to provide pensions, to look after their men when they were too old or ill to work, and to care for their widows when they died. Obedience was required in return. Sir Titus Salt's workers were provided with a school, a chapel, a park, a hospital, and a canteen as well as model houses, but they were forbidden to drink any alcohol, even beer. So were the employees of Sir William Fairbairn, the Scottish-born owner of a Lancashire engineering works, who even insisted that they never appear ill-dressed in the streets in their spare time.

Employers such as Fairbairn worked extremely hard themselves. Not all worked at the pace of George Stephenson, the railway engineer, who rose at dawn, occupied himself with business matters throughout the day, pondered his problems in bed at night, and once dictated, so it was said, for twelve hours running until his secretary almost fell off his chair with exhaustion. Yet many were in their mills at six o'clock in the morning, winter and summer, their daughters riding down at eight to bring their breakfast. The head of the Phillipses' family firm in Manchester preferred to have his breakfast at home in Prestwich; but he had it early, then rode a horse the three miles to Kersal Toll Bar, where a coachman awaited him in a four-wheel cab to take him to his warehouse in the center of the town. After a full day's work he walked back briskly to Kersal Toll Bar, and from there rode home in the dark.

Men like the Phillipses of Manchester and the Gotts of Leeds—enormously rich and influential, acknowledged leaders of industry whose daughters might marry into the aristocracy—were a small elite far removed from most employers in the industrial north.

Only the very largest factories employed more than 200 men, and even these were not to be compared with the big ironworks of South Wales, which employed an average of 650 men each in 1870–71, or a ship-building yard, where work was found for 1,000. Up till the middle of the century the great majority of factories, in-

73

The man with the basket is a Billingsgate fish peddler. Next to him is a chimney sweep and, below him, a flower girl.

deed, were small single-story workshops where ten men or fewer were employed. And even after the development of machines and changes in methods of production, there were still in 1881 no more than 177 persons employed on average in cotton mills and only about 125 in boot and shoe factories.

Small factories, however, were often as disagreeable places in which to work as the dark, satanic mills of early industrial England. William Dodd, who had himself worked in a similar place, described how a typical Manchester factory girl was roused at half past four in the morning by the tap of a watchman's pole on her bedroom window:

At length you hear [the unwilling girl get out of bed and put her feet to] the floor; the clock is striking five, then, for the first time, the girl becomes conscious of the necessity for haste; and having slipped on her clothes, and (if she thinks there is time) washed herself, she takes a drink of cold coffee, which has been left standing in the fireplace, a mouthful of bread (if she can eat it), and having packed up her breakfast in her handkerchief, hastens to the factory. The bell rings as she leaves the threshold of her home. Five minutes more, and she is in the factory. . . . The clock strikes half-past five; the engine starts and her day's work commences.

Two hours later her machine slowed down—it seldom stopped altogether—so that she could clean it and eat her breakfast. After a short time it started up once more and continued at full speed until twelve o'clock, when it stopped. Again she had to clean it before rushing home to have dinner ("which she was seldom able to eat") and to "pack up her drinking for the afternoon." Dodd continued, "This done, it was time to be on her way to work again, where she remains, without a minute's relaxation, till seven o'clock; she then comes home, and throws herself into a chair exhausted. This [is] repeated six days in the week (save that on Saturdays she may get back a little earlier, say, an hour or two). . . . This young woman looks very pale and delicate, and has every appearance of an approaching decline. . . ."

There were factory acts passed that were intended to regulate the conditions of work in mills and to prevent the employment of children; but there were many exceptions and evasions, and the acts were only of limited use in the correction of abuses. Moreover, no sooner had some exploitation of labor been checked in one trade than equally appalling conditions came to light in another. In Yorkshire and Lancashire, in Scotland and Wales, for instance, as the Shaftesbury Commission discovered in 1842, girls and women descended into the coal mines and regularly performed the same kind of underground work for the same number of hours as boys and men, though "a girl of twenty [would] work for two shillings a day or less, and a man of that age would want 3s. 6d."

In great numbers of the coalpits, the commission reported,

74

the men work in a state of perfect nakedness, and are in this state assisted in their labours by females of all ages, from girls of six years old to women of twenty-one, these females being themselves quite naked down to the waist. . . . "One of the most disgusting sights I have ever seen," says the Sub-Commissioner, "was that of young females, dressed like boys in trousers, crawling on all fours, with belts round their waists and chains passing between their legs. . . . In one pit, the chain, passing high up between the legs of two of these girls, had worn large holes in their trousers; and any sight most disgustingly indecent or revolting can scarcely be imagined—no brothel can beat it. On descending Messrs. Hopwood's pit at Barnsley, I found assembled round the fire, boys and girls . . . stark naked down to the waist, their hair bound up with a tight cap, and trousers supported by their hips. Their sex was recognisable only by their breasts, and some little difficulty occasionally arose in pointing out to me which were girls and which were boys, and which caused a good deal of laughing and joking." In [other] pits the system is even more indecent; for . . . at least three-fourths of the men for whom the girls "hurry" work *stark naked*, or with a flannel waistcoat only. [A miner was quoted as saying] "I have worked a great deal where girls were employed in pits. I have had children by them myself, and have frequently had connexion with them in the pits. I am sure that this is the case especially in pits about Lancashire." "I am certain the girls are worse than the men in point of morals [another miner said] and use far more indecent language. . . . I have known myself of a case where a married man and a girl who hurried for him had sexual intercourse often in the bank where he worked." "I have worked in a pit since I was six years old [reported one Betty Wardle]. I have had four children, two of them were born while I worked in the pits. I worked in the pits whilst I was in the family way. I had a child born in the pits, and I brought it up in the pit shaft in my skirt."

A female miner, Betty Harris, aged thirty-seven, described her work in the pits:

I have a belt round my waist, and a chain passing between my legs, and I go on my hands and feet. The road is very steep, and we have to hold by a rope, and when there is no rope by anything we can catch hold of. There are six women and six girls and boys in the pit I work in: it is very hard work for a woman. The pit is very wet where I work, and the water comes over our clog-tops always, and I have seen it up to my thighs; it rains in at the roof terribly; my clothes are wet through almost all day long. . . . My cousin looks

At top is a magazine peddler. The sandwich man could get a shilling and sixpence a day; the boy vendor earned less.

after my children in the daytime. I am very tired when I get home at night; I fall asleep sometimes before I get washed. I am not so strong as I was, and cannot stand my work as well as I used to. I have drawn till I have had the skin off me; the belt and chain is worse when we are in the family way. My feller has beaten me many a time for not being ready. I were not used to it at first, and he had little patience: I have known many a man beat his drawer.

Women and children were prevented from working underground by the Mines and Collieries Act of 1842. But men, women, and children in the chain- and nail-making trades were required to work quite as hard, in conditions almost as bad, for even less money. The men earned at most five shillings a hundredweight, and they were able to produce no more than three hundredweight a week, working a twelve-hour day; while the women often earned less than five shillings a week. "We do not live very well," one of them admitted. "Our most living is bacon." Another, a girl of fifteen, "stated that she did not get enough to eat, even of bread and potatoes." A doctor confirmed that the workers were nearly always hungry.

One of the worst abuses was the masters' habit of forcing the workers to buy their food and other necessities at shops owned by them or by their relations or friends, where prices were very inflated. "They tell their men, or at least it is understood, 'If you do not buy my groceries, we will not buy your nails.'"

The factory inspectors had an impossible task endeavoring to see that the provisions of the factory act were observed, as the masters employed runners to warn of their approach and made it clear that workers who complained of their treatment might well find themselves out of work. Extracts from the act were always found pinned on the workshop wall at the time of the inspectors' visits, only to be stowed back in a drawer as soon as they had gone. Children as well as women were kept at work far into the night as though factory legislation had never been passed. "It is quite a common thing," said a minister from Dudley, a center of the chain-making industry, "for these people to work even thirteen or fourteen hours a day. . . . I have frequently gone through the district, and it is as common as possible to find these people working . . . up to 8 and 9 o'clock at night. In fact, you may go through the district when it is pitch dark, and there are no lamps in some parts, and you will hear these little forges going and people working in them, and you wonder when they are going to stop."

In the chain-making industry, as in every other trade, there was no security for the workingman. It was not only that he could be thrown out of work by the weather—by rain that put a stop to construction of a building or by a contrary wind that kept a ship from docking; it was not only that he could fall ill or suffer some industrial injury for which no employer was obliged to accept responsibility; the whole basis of the law of master and servant before 1875 was weighted heavily against the servant. Men could be prosecuted for breach of contract for refusing to obey the most unreasonable orders and could well find themselves accused of criminal conspiracy if they went on strike—and many were so prosecuted, about ten thousand a year, of whom six thousand were convicted. "What security has the working man?" Engels asked indignantly in 1844. "He knows that, though he may have the means of living today, it is very uncertain whether he shall tomorrow." And although the uncertainty lessened as the Victorian era progressed, the respectable poor were always painfully aware of those "cold, wet, shelterless midnight streets" through which pass the denizens of *Oliver Twist* and in which they themselves might one day be forced to wander.

The miner's life was probably worst of all. Women crawled through long tunnels hauling wagons of ore. Though an early target for reform, mining conditions were still dismal in 1893, when the picture opposite was taken.

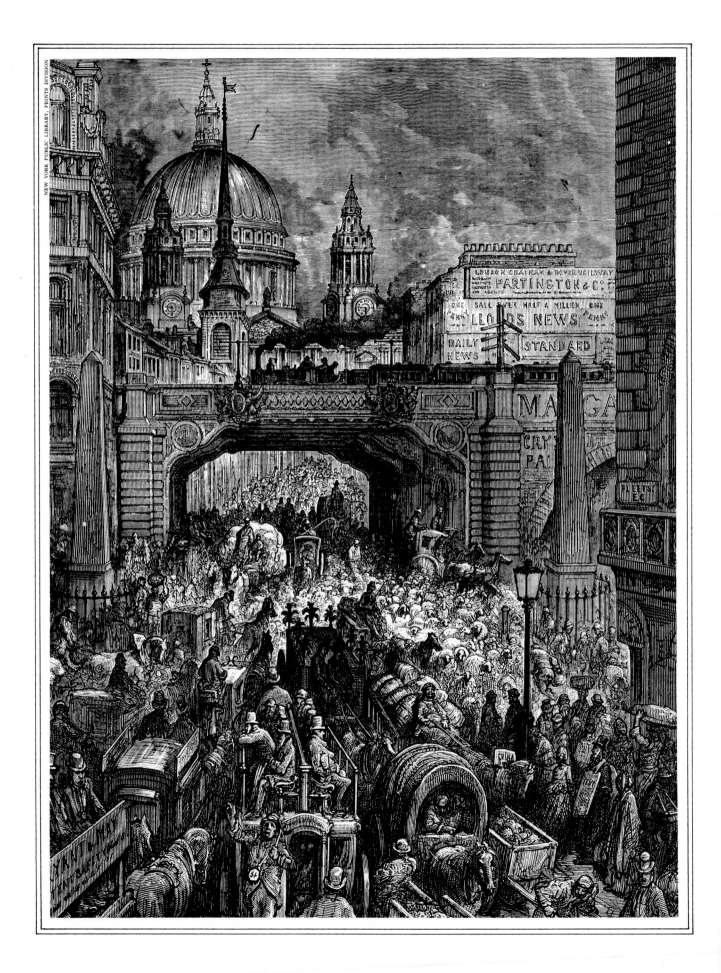

CHAPTER VII

BY THE RAILWAY

"My dear wife Carrie and I have just been a week in our new house, 'The Laurels,' Brickfield Terrace, Holloway —a nice six-roomed residence, not counting basement with a front breakfast-parlour." Thus George and Weedon Grossmith's Mr. Pooter begins his *Diary of a Nobody,* which provides so imperishably vivid a picture of the daily life of a lower-middle-class Victorian family. "We have a little front garden; and there is a flight of ten steps up to the front door, which, by-the-by, we keep locked with the chain up. . . . Our . . . intimate friends always come to the little side entrance, which saves the servant the trouble of going up to the front door, thereby taking her from her work. . . . But Carrie and I can manage to pass our evenings together without friends. There is always something to be done: a tin-tack here, a Venetian blind to put straight, a fan to nail up, or part of a carpet to nail down—all of which I can do with my pipe in my mouth; while Carrie is not above putting a button on a shirt, mending a pillowcase, or practising the 'Sylvia Gavotte' on our new cottage piano (on the three years' system). . . ."

Carrying his umbrella, Mr. Pooter goes up each morning to the City; but he tells us very

CITY MUSEUM AND ART GALLERY, BIRMINGHAM

little about his duties there, confining most of his diary entries to his activities in the evenings at home, where, after enjoying his meat-tea, he reads the newspaper or *Exchange and Mart* and—if there are no odd jobs to do—plays a game of dominoes or bezique with his friend Cummings. Sometimes Mrs. Cummings and other friends call, and they all play consequences or more noisy games, like monkeys and cutlets, or listen to Mrs. Cummings singing a song or Mr. Burwin-Fosselton, of the local amateur dramatic society, the Holloway Comedians, doing his celebrated imitation of Henry Irving. Frequently Pooter's "dear friend" Gowing drops in to have a smoke with him in the breakfast parlor; and one evening Carrie joins them later, but does not stay long, "saying the smoke was too much for her. It was rather too much for me," Mr. Pooter admits, "for Gowing had given me what he called a green cigar, one that his friend Shoemach had just brought over from America. The cigar didn't look green, but I fancy I must have done so; for when I had smoked a little more than half, I was obliged to retire on the pretext of telling Sarah to bring in the glasses."

On a Sunday he and Carrie always go to church, and once the curate came back with them: "I sent Carrie in to open the front door, which we do not use except on special occasions. She could not get it open, and after all my display, I had to take the Curate . . . round to the

As traffic grew and omnibuses came into use, London streets became chaotic. Doré's engraving opposite shows Ludgate Circus in the 1860's. By then the railroad had changed British life, though the ladies above seem bored by its wonders.

side entrance. He caught his foot in the scraper, and tore the bottom of his trousers. Most annoying, as Carrie could not well offer to repair them on a Sunday. After dinner, went to sleep. Took a walk round the garden, and discovered a beautiful spot for sowing mustard-and-cress and radishes. Went to Church again in the evening: walked back with the Curate. Carrie noticed he had got on the same pair of trousers, only repaired. He wants me to take round the plate, which I think a great compliment."

A few days later, having had an argument with the grocer's boy, who had "had the impertinence to bring his basket to the hall-door, and had left the marks of his dirty boots on the fresh-cleaned doorsteps," Mr. Pooter was half an hour late at his office, a thing that had never happened to him in twenty years employment. There has recently been much irregularity in the attendance of the clerks [he records], and Mr. Perkupp, our principal, unfortunately chose this very morning to pounce down upon us early. Someone had given the tip to the others. The result was that I was the only one late of the lot. Buckling, one of the senior clerks, was a brick, and I was saved by his intervention. As I passed by Pitt's desk, I heard him remark to his neighbour: "How disgracefully late some of the head clerks arrive!" This was, of course, meant for me. I treated the observation with silence, simply giving him a look, which unfortunately had the effect of making both of the clerks laugh. Thought afterwards it would have been more dignified if I had pretended not to have heard him at all.

As Mr. Pooter tells us nothing about his daily routine in the City, we have to turn to that other great chronicler of lower-middle-class life, Charles Dickens, to see the clerk at work in his office. Dickens himself was a clerk for a time in the dingy offices of Messrs. Ellis and Blackmore, who occupied "a poor old set of chambers of three rooms," reminiscent of the premises occupied by Mr. Vholes in *Bleak House:*

on so small a scale that one clerk can open the door without getting off his stool, while the other who elbows him at the same desk has equal facilities for poking the fire. A smell as of unwholesome sheep, blending with the smell of must and dust, is referable to the nightly (and often daily) consumption of mutton fat in candles, and to the fretting of parchment forms and skins in greasy drawers. The atmosphere is otherwise stale and close. The place was last painted or whitewashed beyond the memory of man, and the two chimneys smoke, and there is a loose outer surface of soot everywhere, and the dull cracked windows in their heavy frames have but one piece of character in them, which is a determination to be always dirty, and always shut. . . .

The clerks who worked in these offices, as Dickens explained in *Pickwick Papers*, formed one of those numerous small hierarchies within the larger hierarchy of the Victorian social structure. At the top there was the articled clerk, a prospective attorney, who ran up a tailor's bill, received invitations to parties, and knew a family in Gower Street. At the bottom were the middle-aged copying clerks, who had large families and were "always shabby and often drunk," and the office boys, wearing their first overcoats, who "feel a befitting contempt for boys still at day-schools" and, as they went home at night, pooled their pennies for sausages and porter. And in the middle were the salaried clerks, of whom the older generation was respectable and conscientious, like Mr. Pooter, and the younger, a faster set, like Mr. Pooter's egregious son, Lupin, and Richard Swiveller, a clerk to Sampson Brass in *The Old Curiosity Shop*—young men who devoted the major part of their thirty shillings a week to their personal adornment and pleasure, repairing to the Adelphi Theatre at least three times a week and holding court in a cider cellar afterward.

In early Victorian England most of these clerks, like most artisans, went to work on foot, often walking three or four miles each way because the cost of being driven was beyond their limited means. Horse-drawn omnibuses were first seen in 1829; but for many years the fares of the few omnibuses then in commission were beyond the pocket of the average clerk, and it was not until 1846 that the twopence fare was introduced. Thereafter their numbers rapidly increased, and by 1855 they were transporting twenty thousand people to work every day in London alone. By then, indeed, traffic congestion had become a serious problem in most big cities, where, in the morning and evening rush hours, drivers of all manner of vehicles endeavored to find a way through streets already crowded with pedestrians and with men who still chose to ride their horses to work. There were hackneys,

Raffish clerks in a London law office peer down at Mr. Pickwick in an illustration from the Dickens novel drawn by "Phiz."

tilburies, landaus, broughams, and growlers; there were traps and cabriolets; there were Patent Safety Cabs, invented by Joseph Hansom and designed for two passengers whose driver sat behind with the reins going over the roof; there were donkey chaises and pony chaises, dogcarts, caravans, and sociables.

Everyone who could possibly afford it aspired to have his own carriage, since "carriage folk" was a term used to indicate persons of superior social rank, and the possession of a carriage marked an important stage in the social climb of all ambitious men. When Charles Dickens, for example, in the first flush of his success, moved from Doughty Street to a more imposing residence in Regent's Park, his friend John Forster was impressed to notice that at the end of the garden there was a coach house and that it had, instead of the "small chaise with a smaller pair of ponies" with which Dickens had formerly had to be content, a "more suitable equipage," complete with groom. For long journeys abroad Dickens hired "a vast phantom of a travelling coach," in which could be packed his wife, his

sister-in-law, his five children, two nurses, one courier, and the family dog. John Ruskin borrowed a similar—though not quite so large—vehicle for long journeys in England, "a coach hung high, so that we could see well over stone dykes and average hedges out of it," as its contented occupant described it, "such elevation being attained by the old-fashioned folding steps, with a lovely padded cushion fitting into the recess of the door—steps which it was one of my chief delights to see the hostlers fold up and down; though my delight was painfully alloyed by envious ambition to be allowed to do it myself: but I never was—lest I should pinch my fingers."

For long journeys there were also mail coaches and stagecoaches, the fast Exeter Mail Coach covering the 171 miles from London in sixteen and a half hours and the London to Edinburgh coach maintaining an average of 10 miles an hour including stops.

Thomas Telford and John McAdam had long since greatly improved the main roads of England, but journeys were often still very bumpy and the swaying carriages frequently made passengers sick. "Last summer, when we were coming home [to London] from Canterbury, she actually spewed all the way, a distance of sixty miles and not less time than eight hours," one passenger wrote of another.

The people stared as we passed through the towns and villages as she couldent stop even then. It amused me very much to see how the country people stood staring with their mouths half open to see her pumping over the side of the carriage and me sitting by, quite unconcerned, gnawing a piece of cake or some sandwiches or something or other, as her sickness did not spoil my apatite . . . I gave her something to drink every time we changed horses but no sooner than it was down than it came up again.

In the cities steam-driven trams began to be adopted in the 1870's and cable trams in the 1880's. Then came electric trams. The revolutionary proposal to relieve the congestion of traffic in the streets of London by transporting people beneath them was greeted with ridicule and consternation: the houses above the lines would collapse into the tunnels; an enemy army would arrive one day in London by train without

Before the suburban railways came, the commuter had to ride in plodding horse-drawn buses.

anyone knowing it had landed, the duke of Wellington forecast; digging holes in the ground for such a purpose would, in any case, surely be against the laws of God. Despite all protests, however, the tunneling began when enough rich financiers had been persuaded of the venture's profitability. And in May 1862 several dignitaries and their wives, including Mr. and Mrs. William Ewart Gladstone, traveled in open trucks on the first section of the Metropolitan Line. The next year thirty thousand passengers a week were transported underground between Paddington and the City, and several other lines were being planned.

In the early days of the railway the prospect of being driven along an iron track at great speed was extremely alarming to people who had marveled at the twelve miles an hour achieved on patches of good road by the stagecoach to Manchester. When it was learned that the carriages on the London to Woolwich line were to travel half again as fast as that, a journalist protested that he would as soon expect the people of Woolwich to be fired off on a rocket "as trust themselves to the mercy of such a machine going at such a rate." Yet soon after this, trains were racing along at thirty miles an hour, and by 1848 the *Great Britain* was tearing into London at more than a mile a minute.

Most passengers quickly adjusted themselves to these unprecedented speeds. "Riding in an open and shaking carriage so elevated was at first somewhat startling," wrote one of them.

"Dragged along backwards by the snorting engine with such rapidity, under thundering bridges, over lofty viaducts, and through long dark tunnels filled with smoke and steam! By and by, however, we became accustomed even to this."

The queen herself confessed that she actually enjoyed rail travel. "Not quite so fast next time, if you please, Mr. Conductor," Prince Albert was heard to admonish after an early experience on the royal train. But his wife had stronger nerves, admitting, indeed, to being "quite charmed with it" after a railway journey in 1842 from Windsor to London, free from the dust and swaying of a journey by road. Of course, the royal carriages were far more comfortable than those on ordinary trains: there was even a royal lavatory, though this was not available to the queen's ladies, who had to get out when the train stopped for their convenience in lonely places.

The improvements in the comfort and convenience of rail travel did not reconcile everyone to the spread of the iron tracks all over the countryside. Many lamented the spoilation of so much natural beauty; others protested that railways would make revolution more likely, if not inevitable, by enabling the lower orders to move from district to district, spreading dissent; some warned that God's anger would surely fall upon a nation that flouted God's laws; the headmaster of Eton expressed his concern that the locomotives would distract his pupils from their work; and Mrs. Gamp, the gin-loving old nurse and midwife in *Martin Chuzzlewit,* was not alone in her complaints that the "hammering, and roaring, and hissing and lamp-iling . . . sputtering, noisy monsters" of steam engines were no suitable means of transport for any delicate young creatures in their care. "Them Confugion steamers," cries Mrs. Gamp, shaking her umbrella at the Antwerp packet, "has done more to throw us out of our reg'lar work, and bring events on at times when nobody counted on 'em (especially them screeching railraid ones), than all the other frights that ever was took."

The duke of Wellington would have agreed with her. Conservative to the last, he never reconciled himself to "these accursed railroads." In 1838 he was complaining that they had "totally destroyed our convenient communica-

for unskilled work and as much as thirty-three shillings if they could lay bricks or dress stone. But it was dangerous work: 32 men were killed while digging the Woodhead tunnel on the line between Sheffield and Manchester and 540 were injured, many of them seriously. Eating far more meat than most laborers could afford, drinking tions" of Hampshire and "even deranged" the post. Ten years later, having left Chatsworth at six o'clock in the morning to begin his return journey to London on horseback, he was still expressing his decided opinion that

people never acted so foolishly as we did in allowing of the Destruction of our excellent and commodious [post roads] in order to expend Millions Sterling on these Rail Roads! It appears to me to be the Vulgarest, most indelicate, most inconvenient, most injurious to Health of any mode of conveyance that I have seen in any part of the World! Mobs of well dressed Ladies and Gentlemen are collected at every Station, to examine and pry into every Carriage and the actions of every Traveller. If an unfortunate Traveller wishes to quit His Carriage, he is followed by one of these well dressed Mobs as a Hunted animal is by Hounds, till he is forced again in His Carriage!

Despite all protests, however; despite the warning example of the ruin and disgrace of the flamboyant "Railway King," George Hudson, who fled the country leaving investors in companies he had promoted with losses totaling £80,000,000; despite Ruskin's lament for the loss of an idyllic countryside and the demolition of whole areas of old cities for new railway stations, ticket offices, refreshment rooms, engine sheds, repair shops, coal bunkers, and shunting yards, the proliferation of railways continued as fast as ever. More and more numerous armies of laborers, known as navigators—or more usually navvies—because many of them had originally worked on canals, marched across the country to prepare the ground for the long, wide tracks, to dig cuttings, to excavate tunnels, and to build up embankments. They were a rough, tough lot, known to each other by weird nicknames, working hard, ready to move from one part of the country to another, and followed by old women who did their cooking and by younger women who satisfied their other appetites. They were well paid in comparison with other workers, receiving up to twenty-four shillings a week

Thomas Rickett's 1859 steam carriage could lumber along at nineteen miles per hour.

ten pints of strong ale apiece daily and as much other liquor as they could get, they were often drunk, frequently fighting, and a dreaded scourge to the quiet countryside in which they pitched their rowdy camps. "They lived in a state of utter barbarism," wrote John Francis censoriously in 1851.

Some sleep in huts constructed of damp turf . . . others formed a room of stones without mortar and took possession of it . . . often making it a source of profit by lodging as many of their fellow workmen as they crowd into it. . . . In these huts they lived, with the space overcrowded; with man, woman, and child mixing in promiscuous guilt; with no possible separation of the sexes. . . . Drunkenness and dissoluteness of morals prevailed. There were many women, but few wives, loathsome forms of disease were universal. Work often went on without intermission on Sundays as well as on other days.

Navvies had their soft spots, though:

When a working man don't hear anything but swearing, and jeering, and laughing all the week round, for month after month, he can't hardly get it out of his head again rightly [one navvy explained to a journalist]; but, if somebody will come on the works at dinnertime, and read, or talk to us, the men will mostly like it, and be glad to listen. It always does some good, if it is only the being spoken to, now and then, like as if we was the same flesh and blood with other people. We are wonderful tender-hearted, too. A "navvy" will cry the easiest thing as is. If you'll only talk a little good to him, you can make a navvy burst out crying like a child in a few minutes, if you'll only take him the right way.

Beneath the vaulted roof of Paddington Station,
crowds board a train, among them a bride and
groom and boys heading back to school.

While the navvies sweated and drank fortunes were made and lost, and the railway mania
continued unabated. By 1852 there were only a
few market towns and coastal resorts without a
railway station; twenty years later all these had
been provided with one; by 1875 nearly five
hundred million passengers were being transported by rail each year, and the whole tenor of
English life as well as the English landscape had
been transformed. "It was only yesterday," ex-
claims one of Thackeray's characters, "but what a
gulf between now and then. *Then* was the old
world. Stage-coaches, more or less swift riding

horses, packhorses, highwaymen. . . . But your
railroad starts a new era. . . . We who lived before
railways and survive out of the ancient world, are
like Father Noah and his family out of the Ark."

There were advantages as well as regrets.
The railways helped the new towns to grow, and
as they grew, so did the capacity of their inhabitants to enjoy fresh food: the sponsors of the
London to Birmingham line's London terminus
at Euston noted with pride that it was built on
the site of a warren of cowsheds and cow-cellars
from which the nearby households had previously been supplied with tainted and watered
milk instead of the fresh milk that could now be
brought in from the country. Moreover, as it became possible for people to travel beyond the

confines of the enclosed communities from which they had rarely been able to escape before, they discarded their previous suspicions of the outside world and learned both that their fellow countrymen were much like themselves and that social justice was a national concern. It is on a railway journey to Leamington soon after the death of his son, Paul, that Paul Dombey, Sr., realizes the extent of the industrial horrors that he and men like him have allowed to remain undisturbed for so long:

Through the hollow, on the height, by the heath, by the orchard, by the park, by the garden, over the canal, across the river, where the sheep are feeding, where the mill is going, where the barge is floating, where the dead are lying, where the factory is smoking . . . away, with a shriek and a roar and a rattle, and no trace to leave behind but dust and vapour. . . . Louder and louder yet, it shrieks and cries as it comes tearing on. . . . Everything around is blackened. There are dark pools of water, muddy lanes, and miserable habitations far below. There are jagged walls and falling houses close at hand, and through the battered roofs and broken windows, wretched rooms are seen, where want and fever hide themselves in many wretched shapes, while smoke and crowded gables, and distorted chimneys and deformity of brick and mortar penning up deformity of mind and body, choke the murky distance.

As Mr. Dombey looks out of his carriage window, it is never in his thoughts that the monster who has brought him there has let the light of day in on these things, not made or caused them.

Yet although to the reader, if not to Mr. Dombey, the railway is shown as a means of revelation rather than a cause of distress, there are other passages in *Dombey and Son* that vividly describe the changes wrought in Victorian towns by the construction of the railway, for whose unassuageable appetite

houses were knocked down, streets broken through and stopped; deep pits and trenches dug in the ground; enormous heaps of earth and clay thrown up; buildings undermined and shaken, propped by great beams. Here, a chaos of carts, overthrown and jumbled together, lay topsy-turvy at the bottom of a steep unnatural hill; there, confused treasures of iron soaked and rusted in something that had accidentally become a pond. Everywhere were bridges that led nowhere . . . and piles of scaffolding and wildernesses of brick. . . .

Between 1853 and 1885 fifty-six thousand

By the 1870's British rail travel had become comfortable and occasionally elegant. The Pullman dining car at top ran on the Great Northern. Below it is a saloon carriage in 1873.

people were displaced by new railway lines in London alone; and as their houses were demolished, they crowded into already over-populated areas nearby, pouring in hundreds into houses abandoned by the middle classes, who took advantage of the fast and regular train services to move into the spreading suburbs. The South Western Railway's construction of a station at Waterloo completed the degeneration of Waterloo Road from the pleasant, residential area it had been in the earlier decades of the century to mid-Victorian London's most squalid and notorious red-light district.

Still more demolition was carried out when it was decided that the earlier stations—like Isambard Kingdom Brunel's vaulting expanse of wrought iron and glass, which, as a foreign visitor noticed in 1844, had brought into existence a "completely new" district at Paddington—were now too far from the center of the ever-expanding and increasingly populous city. So the later London terminuses, like Victoria and St. Pancras, were built closer to the heart of London, at even greater cost to its inhabitants and character.

As in London, so in the provinces the railway station became one of the principal monuments of the railway age. So did the railway station's indispensable adjunct, the station hotel. Unknown in England before the advent of the railway, the hotel was a Victorian innovation. And there were many who regretted its arrival as much as they deprecated the departure of the old coaching inn. Staying at a new hotel in Brighton in the 1840's, Lord Macaulay protested that the coffeeroom was "ingeniously designed on the principle of an oven" with windows "not made to open, that the dinner comprised yesterday's pease-soup and the day before yesterday's cutlets; not an ounce of ice; and all beverages, wine, water, and beer, in exactly the same state as the Church of Laodicea," neither hot nor cold.

Similar complaints were made about numerous other railway hotels: a meal at the one in Manchester was deemed "inedible"; the station hotel in Birmingham appeared rather to discourage visiting the city than to render a stay there pleasant; the one at Leeds was compared to "an uncomfortable barracks." The author of *London at Table* rather guardedly recommended the Waterloo Hotel as well as the Adelphi and the Bedford, but there were very few places indeed where visitors could dine "not sumptuously, or gluttonously, or licentiously, but plainly and well." There were some good restaurants—the Blue Post, the Café de l'Europe, Dolly's Chophouse, Simpson's, Fenton's, and the Ship and Turtle among them—but foreign visitors lamented the lack of any restaurant or hotel where the cuisine offered much more than the plainest English fare, which most Englishmen themselves considered to be the only food worth eating. "God bless my soul!" the foreign secretary was heard to murmur quietly when dining at the house of the Austrian ambassador. "God bless my soul! No apple pie!"

In the 1860's the hotels began to improve. Offered munificent salaries, several of Europe's greatest chefs and hoteliers came to work in England. The great Escoffier, "King of Chefs and Chef of Kings," came from Monte Carlo to direct the kitchen at the Savoy Hotel, which was built by Richard D'Oyly Carte, the theatrical manager, with the intention of rivaling the best hotels in America; and afterward Escoffier controlled a staff of sixty cooks at the Carlton, where he first introduced menus à la carte. Ritz, later to have a hotel of his own in Piccadilly, also worked at the Savoy; and Alexis Soyer, who had been chef to Prince Polignac in Paris, left the Reform Club, where he had been earning almost £1,000 a year, to open a restaurant at Gore House in Kensington, the former home of the countess of Blessington. Sixty years after this restaurant had closed, an old man's mouth still watered as he remembered the blackcurrant jelly he had eaten there as a schoolboy home for the holidays.

It was not until the railways gave mobility to large numbers of people that the Victorian innovation of the hotel came into being. By the turn of the century, London had many like the imposing Russell in Bloomsbury.

CHAPTER VIII

ON HOLIDAY

In one of his youthful contributions to the *Morning Chronicle*, Charles Dickens described with marvelous verve the bustle and the noise on the road to Greenwich as the people of London, released from their work for the day, drove speedily along in all manner of packed vehicles to enjoy the Easter holiday fair, one of the great delights of early Victorian England. "The dust flies up in clouds, ginger-beer corks go off in volleys"; wheels fly off donkey chaises; girls in rattling coal wagons scream in exaggerated fear to give their admirers cause "to sit remarkably close to them, by way of encouragement"; balconies of public houses are crowded with people smoking and drinking; "half the private houses are turned into tea-shops, fiddles are in great request; every little fruit-shop displays its stall of gilt gingerbread and penny toys; . . . apprentices grow sentimental, and straw-bonnet makers kind."

By the side of the road pedestrians linger in groups, unable to resist the allurements of the "Jack-in-the-box, three shies a penny," or the offers of the Cockney magsman with three thimbles and a pea on a little round board, who cries

© *Country Life*, LONDON

No sportsmen ever looked more stylish than these polo-playing officers of the British army in India. On another level of society the bicycling craze swept through England, presenting a new challenge (above) to the women as well as the men.

out, "Here's the sort o' game to make you laugh seven years arter you're dead, and turn ev'ry 'air on your 'ed gray with delight! Three thimbles and vun little pea—with a vun, two, three and a two, three, vun: catch him who can, look on, keep your eyes open, and niver say die! . . . all fair and above board: them as don't play can't vin, and luck attend the royal sportsman! Bet any gen'l'm'n any sum of money, from harf-a-crown up to a suverin, as he doesn't name the thimble as kivers the pea!"

In the park gypsies tell fortunes; pensioners sell glimpses through their telescopes of the river and the places where pirates used to hang in chains; and pretty girls are dragged up the steep hill and then dragged down again at top speed, "greatly to the derangement of their curls and bonnet-caps, and much to the edification of lookers-on from below." And inside the fairground are stalls of gingerbread, toy whistles, and spice nuts, where "unbonneted young ladies, in their zeal for the interest of their employers," grab potential customers by the coat "and use all the blandishments of 'Do, dear'—'There's a love'—Don't be cross, now.'" There are tables, too, spread with pickled salmon in little white saucers, oysters and whelks, and cigars at two a penny "in a regular authentic cigar-box, with a lighted tallow candle in the centre." The air is filled with "the shouts of boys, the clanging of

89

Despite the fact that the beasts were unpredictable, many street performers kept trained bears.
The Saturday Book, 1945

gongs, the firing of pistols, the ringing of bells, the bellowings of speaking-trumpets . . . the noise of a dozen bands, with three drums in each, all playing different tunes at the same time, the hallooing of showmen, and an occasional roar from the wild-beast shows" outside, where the lion tamer, a very tall, hoarse man in a scarlet coat, informs the passers-by that his most "fe-ro-cious lion . . . has killed on the average three keepers a-year ever since he arrived at matoority. No extra charge on this account, recollect; the price of admission is only sixpence."

As well as lions and tigers that would tear men's heads open as soon as look at them, there are giantesses and living skeletons; a wild Indian and a "young lady of singular beauty, with perfectly white hair and pink eyes"; a military band in beefeaters' costumes and leopard-skin caps; and a dwarf, "who is always particularly drunk" and sings a comic song inside a doll's house.

The biggest booth has a large stage in front of it; and here are performed melodramas ("with three murders and a ghost"), pantomimes and comic songs, "an overture, and some incidental music, all done in five-and-twenty minutes." And the noisiest place of all is the dancing booth, where the heat is insupportable and the women dance in men's hats and the men in women's bonnets, wearing false noses and banging on children's drums.

At this time most men in full employment worked six long days a week. So holidays like this were precious times to be enjoyed to the full. Saturday afternoons off were unknown until a factory act of 1850 introduced them in the textile industry. But once they had become established in textile workshops, they soon spread to other trades; and although it was to take a further generation before the eight-hour working day became common, in the second half of the century working hours shortened sufficiently for laborers and artisans to enjoy their leisure with a new enthusiasm.

Thomas Wright, an author from a working-class background, described how eagerly the men waited for the one o'clock bell on a Saturday in Manchester; how they relished being able to stroll home unhurriedly to their dinner; how, after dinner, they smoked their pipes "still in a leisurely and contemplative manner unknown to them at other times"; how they would then go down to the public baths, taking their clean clothes with them to put on when they had washed and bringing away their working suits tied up in a bundle.

Their clean clothes, so Wright said, usually consisted of moleskin or cord trousers, black coat and waistcoat, "a cap of somewhat sporting character, and a muffler more or less gaudy." Thus attired, some sat down to read the papers; others went shopping with their wives and considered the afternoon well spent if they succeeded in beating down a butterman to the extent of three halfpence; yet others went for an afternoon stroll round the town, "much given to gazing in at shop windows—particularly of newsagents, where illustrated papers and periodicals are displayed," and of outfitters where there could be seen "those great bargains in gorgeous and fashionable scarfes marked up at the sacrificial price of 1s. 11¾d."

Many men were members of workshop bands and went booming about the town with trombone, bassoon, and trumpet; many more changed into cheerful uniforms and went to parade proudly up and down suburban fields with the local volunteer corps. Hundreds of men spent their

Beneath a wall thickly papered with advertisements, Barnum and Bailey Circus parades through a Bristol street in the summer of 1898.
THE REECE WINSTONE COLLECTION

Saturday afternoons betting on greyhound races. And toward the end of the century, having taken back the game from the public schools, which had borrowed it from them, thousands went to play soccer or paid to watch matches between professional teams. In the summer families took picnics and went out into the country, for open fields were within walking distance of every town. It was, for example, but two and a half miles to Kersal Moor from the center of Manchester, and filthy though the city center was, the air was clear on the moor and the river water was clean enough to bathe in.

William Powell Frith's teeming Derby Day *was exhibited at the Royal Academy in 1858. The painting was so popular that special railings were needed to keep back the crowds.*

However they spent their Saturday afternoons, Wright continued, his friends contrived to bring them to an early conclusion so as to leave themselves a long evening, preferably at the theatre, the music hall, or the public house.

The theatre is the most popular resort of pleasure-seeking workmen, and the gallery their favourite part of the house. Two or three mates generally go together taking with them a joint-stock bottle of drink and a suitable supply of eatables. Or sometimes two or three married couples who have "no encumbrance," or who have got some neighbour to look after their children, make up a party. . . . The eating and drinking that goes on in the gallery may appear to be mere gluttony, though the fact really is that it is a simple necessity. There is scarcely a theatre gallery in England from the back seats of which it is possible to see and hear with any degree of comfort, or in a manner

that will enable you to comprehend the action of the piece without standing during the whole of the performance, and standing up in a gallery crowd is a thing to be contemplated with horror. In order to get a place . . . from which you can witness the performance while seated, it is necessary to be at the entrance at least half an hour before the doors open, and when they do open you have to take part in a rush and struggle the fierceness of which can only be credited by those who have taken part in such encounters. . . . [Moreover] the refreshments . . . provided by the theatrical purveyors of them, being of a sickly and poisonous . . . character, consisting for the most part of ale and porter, originally bad, and shaken in being carried about until it has become muddy to the sight and abominable to the taste; rotten fruit, and biscuits stale to the degree of semi-putrefaction; those . . . who take a supply of refreshments with them when they go to a theatre, display, not gluttony, but a wise regard for their health and comfort.

The theatre was equally popular in London, where there were performances to suit all tastes. There was Shakespeare at Sadler's Wells; Donizetti at Covent Garden; modern dramas at the Haymarket; comedies, farces, operettas, and burlettas at a score of places from Drury Lane to the Mile End Road. At Astley's in Westminster Bridge Road the management presented an extraordinarily diverse fare, including melodramas, circus clowns, acrobats, sword fights, elephants, and performing horses. It is here that Kit Nubbles took his family.

What a place it looked, that Astley's! With all the paint, gilding and looking-glass, the vague smell of horses suggestive of coming wonders, the clean white sawdust down in the circus, the company coming in

and taking their places, the fiddlers looking carelessly up at them while they tuned their instruments, as if they didn't want the play to begin, and knew it all beforehand! What a glow was that which burst upon them all, when that long, clear, brilliant row of lights came slowly up. . . . Then the play itself! The horses, the firing . . . the forlorn lady . . . the tyrant . . . the pony who reared up on his hind legs when he saw the murderer . . . the clown who ventured on such familiarities with the military man in boots . . . the lady who jumped over the nine and twenty ribbons and came down safe upon the horse's back.

Then there were the music halls, offering equally diverse programs of operatic arias, comic and patriotic songs, romantic ballads, and —for many patrons the principal attraction— pretty barmaids behind long counters, where the younger members of the audience chose to stand, drinking, smoking, making lewd comments, and joining in the choruses of the songs. Above all, there were the theatres on the south bank of the river, where the more melodramatic the plot and the more violent the action, the greater was the audience's delight. The most popular of these was the Coburg, better known as the Vic. When a new play was announced here, crowds thronged outside long before the doors were opened.

"To the centre of the road, and all round the door, the mob is in a ferment of excitement," so the readers of the *Morning Chronicle* were informed, "and no sooner is the money-taker at his post than the most frightful rush takes place, every one heaving with his shoulder at the back of the person immediately in front of him. The girls shriek, men shout, and a nervous fear is felt lest the massive staircase should fall in with the weight of the throng, as it lately did with the most terrible results." As many as two thousand people could be crammed onto the benches of the gallery, and inside the noise was tremendous. Costermongers in shirt sleeves and "black-faced sweeps or whitey-brown dustmen" bawled greetings and insults to one another and amused themselves by pitching orange peels and nut-shells at the bonnets of the women, many of whom had brought their babies with them.

Fierce arguments erupted and fights were common, yet at the rising of the curtain the hubbub suddenly subsided with shouts for silence and order. Throughout the performance the spectators munched pig trotters and ham sandwiches, which were sold in the frequent intervals, sucked oranges, cracked nuts, drank porter, greeted complaints that the people behind could not see with threats to throw them over the railings, wiped the sweat from their faces with crumpled-up playbills, shouted at the actors to speak up, and encouraged them with cries of "Bray-vo, Vincent! Go to it, my tulip!"

No delay between the pieces will be allowed, and should the interval appear too long, some one will shout out—referring to the curtain—"Pull up that there winder blind!" or they will call to the orchestra, saying, "Now then you catgut-scrapers! Let's have a ha'purth of liveliness." Neither will they suffer a play to proceed until they have a good view of the stage, and "Higher the blue," is constantly shouted, when the sky is too low, or "Light up the moon," when the transparency is rather dim.

The dances and comic songs, between the pieces, are liked better than anything else. A highland fling is certain to be repeated, and a stamping of feet will accompany the tune, and a shrill whistling, keep time through the entire performance. But the grand hit of the evening is always when a song is sung to which the entire gallery can join in the chorus.

The gallery was almost always full; and if a member of the audience left before the performance was over, he would immediately be surrounded by a crowd of boys who habitually clustered at the foot of the staircase begging for return checks, which they would then sell for 1½d. or 1d., according to the lateness of the hour. Admittance could also be gained for 1d. to those numerous shops turned into temporary theatres and known as penny gaffs. Here there were displays of "flash dancing," in which "the most disgusting attitudes were struck," in the words of one harsh critic of these establishments, and "the most immoral acts represented"; comic songs, "the whole point of which consisted in the mere utterance of some filthy word at the end of each stanza"; and—between the acts—public dancing, the couples, mostly boys and girls from eight years old to twenty, moving about "grotesquely, to the admiration of the lookers-on,

Boating on the Thames was a popular pastime. Edward J. Gregory's painting shows a great variety of craft crowding their way through Boulter's Lock at Maidenhead, above London.

95

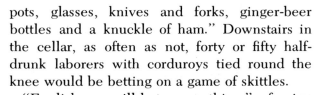

Dressed in what they regarded as proper mountain gear, an English climbing party makes its way up Mont Blanc. In the 1865 photograph opposite, the Curtis family plays croquet in their garden at Alton, Hampshire.

who expressed their approbation in obscene terms that, far from disgusting the poor little women, were received as compliments, and acknowledged with smiles and coarse repartees. The boys clustered together, smoking their pipes, and laughing at each other's anecdotes, or else jingling halfpence in time with the tune. . . ."

The performance over, the audience would pour out again into the street, shouting and laughing, the boys jumping onto the girls' shoulders, the girls giggling hysterically as they were tickled and pinched by the fingers behind them. They would then, perhaps, make for a public house or one of those garish gin-shops, behind whose fantastically ornamented parapet, illuminated clock, and plate-glass windows were elaborately carved bars of French mahogany, lighted by glittering chandeliers and attended by showily dressed girls with painted faces and ornamented bosoms. Enclosed within a bright brass rail were row upon row of green and gold casks of gin, bearing such enticing names as "The Out and Out," "The No Mistake," "The Real Knock-Me-Down," or "Samson." Such spirits were also to be bought in so-called coffee shops, on whose long counters, amid the bottles of liquor and the jars of rum, a visitor might have found "many loaves of bread, flitches of bacon, a quantity of butter, two tea-urns (unpolished and out of use), three beer-pumps for Kop's ale, and a glass jar filled with pickled onions, together with a great debris of mustard

pots, glasses, knives and forks, ginger-beer bottles and a knuckle of ham." Downstairs in the cellar, as often as not, forty or fifty half-drunk laborers with corduroys tied round the knee would be betting on a game of skittles.

"Englishmen will bet on anything," a foreign visitor observed, and one of the most popular forms of gambling was betting at a rat match. There were about forty taverns in mid-Victorian London, and at least one in every provincial town, where dogs were set upon rats in a special pit and where bets were placed on the terriers fancied to kill the greatest number. The pit was a small arena with a white-painted floor surrounded by a wooden rail. The rats were tossed into it from a rusty iron cage by a man whose experience allowed him to thrust his arm into the struggling mass and grab hold of the "varmints" by their tails. When about fifty animals had been flung into the pit, in which they gathered themselves into a pullulating mound, a wheezing and screaming would be heard in the passage outside and a boy would come in "carrying in his arms a bull-terrier in a perfect fit of excitement, foaming at the mouth and stretching its neck forward so that the collar which held it back seemed to be cutting its throat in two."

The moment the dog was released he suddenly became quiet, then rushed at the rats, burying his nose in the mound until he brought one out in his mouth. A stopwatch recorded the minutes allowed for each match; and when the time was

up, the dead rats were picked up and flung into a pile in the corner, and the landlord would invite the spectators to "give their minds up to drinking" before the next contest began.

For those who had no money to spare for drinking or betting there were the endless diversions of the streets. There were conjurers and fire-eaters; Punch and Judy shows; acrobats and strong men; jugglers and swallowers of knives, snakes, and swords; clowns and dancing dogs; gymnastic monkeys and tightrope dancers; stilt vaulters; reciters; hurdy-gurdy players; street bands; organ grinders; ballad singers; Negro serenaders; fantoccini men, who manipulated dancing dolls and jangling skeletons; and exhibitors of birds and mice, mechanical figures, waxworks, telescopes, and peepshows. Many of these showmen would accept an empty bottle from an urchin who had no money, and all of them were used to seeing half their audience slink away before the collection began.

I cut the sweep trade and started with an organ-man, as his mate, [a former climbing boy, recalled]. I saved money with the organ-man and then bought a drum. He gave me five shillings a week and my wittles and drink, washing and lodging. . . . Then I left the music-man [and went out with an Italian, called Michael, who had a performing bear]. He used to beat the bear and manage her; they called her Jenny; but Michael was not roughish to her unless she was obstropelous. If she were he showed her the large mop-stick, and beat her with it—hard sometimes, specially when she wouldn't let the monkey get a top on her head; for that was a part of the performance. The monkey was dressed the same as a soldier . . . a clever fellow he was, and could jump over sticks like a Christian and was called Billy. He jumped up and down the bear, too, and on his master's shoulders where he set as Michael walked up and down the streets. The bear had been taught to roll and tumble. She rolled right over her head, all round a stick, and then she danced round about it . . . . Sometimes the butchers set bull-dogs, two or three at a time at Jenny; and Michael and me had to beat them off as well as the other two men that we had with us. Those two men collected the money, and I played the pipes and drum, and Michael minded the bear and the monkey and the dogs that jumped through hoops and danced on their hind legs. In London we did very well. The West End was the best. Whitechapel [in the East End] was crowded for us, but only with ha'pence. I don't know what Michael made but I had seven shillings a week, with my wittles and lodging. . . . We generally had twenty to thirty shillings every night in ha'pence . . . when we've travelled in the country, we've sometimes had trouble to get lodgings for the bear. We've had to sleep in outhouses with her, and have sometimes frightened people that didn't know as we was there, but nothing serious. Bears is well behaved enough if they ain't aggravated. The country was better than London when the weather allowed; but in Gloucester, Cheltenham, and a good many places we weren't let in the high streets. . . . Michael and me parted at Chester . . . and I drummed and piped my way to London, and there took up with another foreigner in the clock-work-figure line. The figures danced on a table when taken out of a box. Each had its own dance when wound up.

After the excitement of a Saturday night, Sunday mornings were quiet, the streets disturbed only by the occasional cry of a costermonger, the shops mostly shut, the women getting ready to go out to the street markets, the men repairing their rabbit hutches and pigeon lofts or lying in bed reading *Lloyd's Weekly Newspaper* while waiting for the public houses to open. In the afternoons those who had not drunk too much and retired to bed again after dinner took their families for a walk in a park or a pleasure-garden, for a ride on a tram to visit relations, or for a trip down the river on a steamboat. For a special treat the more enterprising and better off might have gone to the railway station to make an excursion into the country or even to the seaside.

"Have been this morning and had a bathe in the sea for the first time," a footman recorded

Gilbert and Sullivan cheerfully satirized British life in operettas such as The Mikado.

in his diary while his employers were on holiday at Brighton.

I like it very much . . . I go to the seaside two or three times a day and amuses myself by seeing the pleasure boats or seeing the fishermen come in with their vessils of fish, or sometimes I stand and watch the large waves jump over the small ones. . . . There are many things to be seen here. Brighton is a very pleasant place. . . . I get up every morning at half past six and goes out on the beach, looking at the boys catching crabs and eels and looking at the people batheing. There are numbers of old wimen have little wooden houses on wheels, and into these houses people go that want to bathe, and then the house is pushed into the water and when the person has undressed, they get into the water and bathe, and then get into the wooden house again and dress themselves, then the house is drawn on shore again.

With the opening of the railway from London in 1841, Brighton ceased to be the fashionable place it had been in the days of the Regent, who had made it so. The beach was for people who came down for the day: for children with shrimping nets and parents with hampers of buns and pies and bottles of ginger beer, for brass bands and donkey rides, for cheeky young men with fancy waistcoats and giggling girls. It was, in fact, as one aloof visitor commented, a place for *hoi polloi*.

For the middle classes the seaside resorts of the southeast and the northwest held a fascination that they were never to lose. Writing in 1864, the artist Richard Doyle thought that the sandy beaches of Kent had surely been made for children. "How fresh and handsome they look, the splendid brave-looking little fellows, in their sailor-hats and jackets, the sun shining upon their bright, round, red cheeks, and the pretty little chubby girls with their long hair flying about in the breeze. What intense happiness to dabble up to their ankles in the sea! What delight to dig canals with the little spades, and to build up great castles of sand! What fun to bury one another, and how jolly to dig one another up again, and what a gratification to spoil one another's clothes."

Bathing was considered more of a duty than a pleasure. Sea water was known to be so health-giving that doctors recommended drinking it, "mixed with port wine, milk or beef tea to make it more palatable," as well as immersing the body in it with the help of a dipper, whose duty it was to insure that the timid did not shrink from plunging head and body beneath the waves. Up till the 1870's in most resorts it was still the practice for men to bathe naked. In 1872 Francis Kilvert, the Wiltshire curate, found "a delicious feeling of freedom in stripping in the open air [on the sands at Weston-super-Mare] and running down naked to the sea, where the waves were curling white with foam and the red morning sunshine glowing upon the naked limbs of the bathers." But two years later, at Shanklin on the Isle of Wight, Kilvert found that it was no longer considered proper to go into the sea unclothed: men were now expected to adopt what Kilvert called the detestable custom of wearing drawers, and by the 1890's even drawers were considered immodest and had been replaced by bathing costumes with three-quarter-length sleeves and legs reaching to the knees.

Ladies dressed themselves in heavy serge with elbow-length sleeves and baggy bloomers concealed by thick, full skirts. And before the adoption of the Continental custom of the striped tent, they were transported out to sea in a lurching wooden hut, which was pulled by an antiquated horse and turned round when the water was waist-high. The door, often screened from the beach by a hood, was then opened; and the bather was approached by the dipper, an intimidating woman, usually fat and frequently drunk, who was clothed in waterproof wrappings and a large bonnet.

98

The crowded beach at Ramsgate was immortalized by W. P. Frith in his picture *Life at the Seaside.* Children are shown paddling and digging in the sand with wooden spades; men read newspapers or peer out to sea through telescopes; and women, in their straw bonnets and crinolines, shaded by their parasols from the harmless rays of the pale sun, work at their embroidery, look at books, pretend not to look at exhibitors of trained mice, and studiedly ignore the men selling whelks and ships in bottles. Behind them Negro minstrels dance and sing and play banjos; a Punch and Judy man beats his drum to attract children to the next drama of Jack Ketch the hangman, the Blind Man, and Toby the dog; and little girls stand on tiptoe to watch the antics of a performing rabbit.

Frith's *Derby Day* (pages 92-93) depicts with equal realism an afternoon on Epsom Downs, one of the few places where the upper classes did not disdain the company of the lower. There is the inevitable magsman with his thimbles and his pea, the dejected apprentice who has lost his bet, the barefooted bookie's assistant shouting the odds, the unkempt gypsy children watching the acrobats, and the acrobats' small son in doublet and tights looking wistfully at a fine picnic of turkey pie and lobster, which is being laid out on the grass for a party of rich-looking ladies and gentlemen in the carriage behind him. In other carriages gentlemen drink wine and ladies study their race cards while a smart little gentleman in a velvet suit and frilled lace collar leans over the hood to drop a penny into a battered hat held up to him by a beggarwoman with a baby in her arms.

"The first thing that particularly struck me was the mixed character of the multitude," wrote an American clergyman who had got caught up in the crowd and found himself on Epsom Downs by mistake.

Kindred tastes had brought together . . . the extremes of society into the closest contact. Here were the carriages of the nobility, emblazoned with their appropriate coat of arms and attended by liveried footmen. . . . In the same throng were the very off-scouring of the earth, clad in rags and squalidness. In the same group, or standing near each other, might have been seen high-born ladies, servant girls, gypsies and the most worthless of the sex all pressing forward to

The Levey sisters, shown on the cover of one of their song sheets, were a highly successful music-hall team during the 1890's.

witness the races. . . . In the interval between the races, the course ground was filled with rope-dancers, jugglers, necromancers and various kinds of gamesters.

For those with a taste for more violent sports, there was prize fighting, which, though not as popular as it had been in the first quarter of the century, still attracted crowds—as at Farnborough in 1860, when spectators traveled in special trains to see Tom Sayers, the small and doughty English champion, knocked down repeatedly by the huge American John C. Heenan in a drawn fight of thirty-seven rounds that lasted over two hours.

Condemnation of such brutal contests was, however, growing ever stronger, and Victorian gentlemen were far more likely to be found beside the cricket field or on the rugby pitch than hanging round a boxing ring. Cricket had formerly been a rough game played on village greens by countrymen without too nice a regard for even local rules; it was "the common pastime

99

of the common people." But the public schools and the emergence of first-class amateurs—of whom the large, bearded doctor W. G. Grace was the most celebrated example—helped to alter the status of the game, which became almost synonymous with a gentlemanly code of conduct. Rugby, too, except in South Wales and in the north, was a gentleman's game—invented at the public school, played with an oval ball, and, toward the end of the century, known at Oxford and Cambridge and thereafter everywhere as rugger—in contradistinction to soccer, that inferior form of football, the pastime of artisans and yokels.

As the century progressed, and organized ball games with established rules became an essential part of the public-school ethos, new games were invented and old ones modernized. Lawn tennis, an adaptation of the medieval game played in an enclosed court, was patented in 1874 by an English Army officer; polo was introduced from India in 1869; golf was borrowed from the Scots and by 1885 was considered a game mastered well enough by women for them to be admitted to men's full courses; croquet came over from France by way of Ireland and soon became one of the most popular games of all, since it could be played by men and women of all ages and on the lawn in nearly every middle-class garden.

Getting wet at the seashore was no simple process: one climbed into a bathing machine, which was then pulled out into the surf. Picnics like the one at right were the inland counterparts of a day at the beach.

GERNSHEIM COLLECTION, UNIVERSITY OF TEXAS, AUSTIN

RADIO TIMES HULTON PICTURE LIBRARY

CHAPTER IX

THE UNDERWORLD

Compelled to leave his home by a railway company intent upon pulling it down in order to lay a new track, Thomas Wright, a respectable but temporarily unemployed workingman, was forced to take his family to live on one of those crowded courts, where, as he said, crime and misery jostled each other, disease was rife, children had to be well guarded if they were not to be corrupted, and "any latent disposition to depravity and vice" would surely be "fostered and developed." His neighbors were hawkers; rag-and-bone collectors; baked-potato sellers; washerwomen; prostitutes; a "wild Irish family"; and numerous men who called themselves laborers, who never seemed to have any regular employment, did not get up until ten or eleven o'clock in the morning, could usually be seen loafing about street corners during the afternoon, yet who always had money to spend on tobacco and gambling and on drinking in the public houses, which they occupied until a late hour at night.

In every large city there were thousands of men like these, living wholly or partly on the proceeds of crime. They were street thieves and pickpockets, footpads and shoplifters; pimps and

THE GUILDHALL LIBRARY, LONDON

Crime and depravity flourished in the warrens of the poor. In Gustave Doré's engraving opposite a policeman with a bull's-eye lantern makes his rounds. The man above, masked for the sake of anonymity, is an inmate of Pentonville Prison.

whores' bullies; bug-hunters, who made a practice of robbing drunks; shofulmen, who were expert in passing counterfeit money; sneaksmen, who dipped their nimble fingers into carriage windows; snoozers, who emerged from hotel rooms to rob their fellow guests; and all those other types of petty criminal who lived by plunder, cheating, and, sometimes when occasion demanded, by violence.

Many of them had been born and bred in rookeries and had started out in life as infant thieves, working for some fence, such as Taff Hughes — a far more terrifying figure than Dickens's Fagin — who would turn in fury on any of his little brood who came back empty-handed and flog him with the strap that held his wooden leg on. Others had begun as assistants to a beggar, representing themselves as the pathetic offspring of a shipwrecked sailor, a crippled soldier, a tubercular miner, or a fallen woman, earning a penny a day for following their master or mistress about in tears and in rags. Some had come in from the country, where they had tramped the roads for months in search of work, pilfering and begging on the way and occasionally peering menacingly through cottage windows and exacting money by threats.

This is the way we used to carry on [recalled one of those numerous agricultural laborers who had left their farms to tramp in search of better-paid work]. Perhaps I'd light on an old mate somewhere about the country, and we'd go rambling together from one place to another. If we earned any money, we'd go to a public house, and stop there two or three days, till we'd spent it all or till the publican turned us all out drunk and helpless to the world. Having no money to pay for a lodging, we had to lie under a hedge, and in the morning we'd get up thinking "What shall we do?" "Where shall we go?" . . . We'd wander on till we could find a gang of men at work at some railroad or large building; sometimes they would help us and sometimes they would not. Once I travelled about for three days without having anything to eat. We'd always sooner take a thing than ask for it . . . and seeing some poor labouring man's victuals lying under a hedge, I jumped over and took them . . . I got some work in Sussex. I got four shillings a day, working Sundays and all. I bid there eleven weeks till I had saved nine pounds and then I left to come to London by train. There I got along with bad company, and spent three or four of my pounds, and then turned towards Derby where I spent the rest of my money and had to lie again in a stable. From there I walked into Yorkshire.

While I was in Yorkshire I met with a young gentleman who had a fine house of his own, but he would spend all his time in the beer-shop. One day he saw me there and called out, "Well, old navvy.... Can you drink a quart of ale? . . . Well if you will stop along of me, I'll keep you in drink, as long as you like to sing me songs."

"Master," says I, "I'll have you! I do like my beer."

I stopped at the public-house with the young gentleman, holloing and shouting and drinking, and up to all sorts of wild pranks. He could not abide to be left alone, because of the "blue devils," as we call them. He had been drunk every day for three months, so he would do anything to get someone to keep him company. I stopped with him a fortnight drinking Yorkshire ale at 6 pence a quart, while he drank rum and brandy, and soda water, between whiles. . . . But at the fortnight's end I had to run away. I could not stand it any longer. He'd have killed me with it, if I'd gone on. . . . It was not long after this that I got sent to prison.

This man drifted into crime. The journalist John Binny interviewed another who seems to have chosen criminality as a way of life. His story provides an illuminating account of a petty thief's career. The son of a nonconformist preacher in Shropshire, he ran away from home as a young boy and went to London, where he met a gang of little pickpockets who lived in the battered shell of a prison van under the arches of the Adelphi and sold silk handkerchiefs they had stolen from gentlemen's pockets to an intimidating fence named Larry. He joined the gang, and although he became an extremely adept pickpocket, he was soon caught in the act and sent to prison for two months.

On his discharge he was met by two smartly dressed young men who had learned of his prowess and who took him away with them to a house in Flower-and-Dean Street, Whitechapel, where he was trained to pick ladies' pockets, practicing on the mistress of one of his mentors. Provided with fashionable black mourning clothes and a beaver hat, he was deemed expert enough after three days practice to go out with three other elegantly dressed pickpockets to show what he could do. All four of them went to a pastry cook's in St. Paul's Churchyard to spot a suitable victim among the customers. They followed a lady out, and the boy neatly took her purse while she was looking in a hosier's window, quickly passing it on to one of his companions. The operation was successfully repeated three times that day; and on almost every subsequent day for weeks he and his accomplices went out tooling, as they called it, until he was caught again, arrested, and sent for three months to the Blackfriars Bridewell. Immediately on his release he went back to the gang and for over three years pursued his craft uninterruptedly, stealing from women not only in the streets but also in church, at fairs and pleasure-gardens, at Madame Tussaud's, at the zoo, and at the theatre. One Derby Day he was nearly caught on Epsom Downs but was saved by the intervention of one of his accomplices, who went to prison for four months himself.

He was still only twelve, so he said; but that year he took a mistress three years older than himself and lived with her in some style, wearing smart clothes and carrying plenty of money in his pocket, until the girl ran away from him because he beat her. Not long afterward he was arrested again and sentenced to a further term of imprisonment; on coming out, he decided that he was too well known in his old haunts and went to work with new accomplices in a different locality. But again he was arrested and imprisoned and, having lost his former associates,

Sanguinary line cuts from The Illustrated Police News, *a popular weekly, depict crimes of the year 1860: a policeman being shot and a wife about to be axed in her bedroom.*
BOTH: *Illustrated Police News*

went to work on his own, stealing men's watches. Less adept at this than at tooling women, he was caught and sent to prison once more.

When he got out, he went back to work with a gang stealing from women, and for several years he was highly successful, despite occasional misfortunes that landed him in prison but never for more than twelve months. Not once were his earlier convictions brought up before sentence was passed. At the great Chartist rally at Kensington in 1848 he lifted a pocketbook containing £135, and he did almost as well at the Great Exhibition in 1851. But thereafter his fortunes declined. Determined to rise in the criminal hierarchy and become a burglar, he cast in his lot with two inexperienced cracksmen, who took him with them to rob a building in the City, which they mistakenly supposed to be unoccupied during the afternoon. The alarm being given, he endeavored to escape but was knocked down by a passer-by, who hit him over the head with an umbrella. He was sentenced to imprisonment in Holloway Prison, where he was put into

solitary confinement, a punishment that so greatly undermined his health and confidence that he was never afterward successful as a pickpocket and was driven, prematurely aged at thirty-one, to making an uncertain living by petty thieving and selling broadsheets in the streets.

Had he succeeded as a burglar, he would have been able to live far more comfortably than he had ever done as a swell mobsman. Indeed, some burglars, so Binny recorded, kept servants, drank the choicest wines, bought the most expensive clothes for their women, invested their profits, and eventually retired to become publicans or proprietors of a few hansom cabs. They lived in perfectly respectable districts far removed from those nightmarish criminal slums, where fights between screaming, drunken women with black eyes and bandaged noses would call forth the inhabitants of the adjacent lanes "like a human sewer suddenly discharging its contents."

The most experienced and clever cracksmen were highly skilled technicians, expert in the handling of the finest tools of their craft and capable of planning the most ambitious crimes. One such crime was carefully devised by two professional felons, Pierce and Agar, a daring scheme to steal a consignment of gold coins and ingots worth many thousands of pounds while in transit from London to Paris on a train of the South Eastern Railway Company. After several months of preparation, during which they managed to corrupt both a guard and a clerk of the company's traffic department, they cleverly obtained duplicate keys of the heavy steel cases in which the gold was to be locked during the journey. On a day when the suborned guard was on duty, Pierce and Agar, quietly and expensively dressed, bought first-class tickets to Folkestone and deposited several couriers' bags filled with bags of lead-shot in the guard's van. Unlocking the steel cases during the journey, they took out the gold, which they placed in their couriers' bags, substituting the lead-shot. When the train arrived at Folkestone, they took their bags across the platform and entered the train for Dover, where, having previously bought tickets for the crossing from Ostend, they were able to give the impression that they had just come over from the Continent; and so they returned to London. They would probably have got away with the crime had not Agar's mistress betrayed them eighteen months later.

If they had been given sufficient warning of their betrayal and taken shelter in one of those criminal strongholds into which hunted men could retreat and disappear, they might never have been found. For in every large city, and most notoriously in London, Manchester, and Birmingham, there were extraordinary enclaves protected by ferocious guard dogs from the attentions of authority and inhabited almost entirely by gangs of criminals and their women and children. In these mazes of courts—where rotting bridges spanned noisome ditches, where walls "the colour of bleached soot" leaned inward over darkened alleyways, where windows, whose shattered panes were filled with bits of blackened board and filthy straw, and splintered doors creaked on rusty hinges—holes were cut through walls and ceilings into cellars and out of roofs so that a criminal fearing arrest could soon escape from his pursuers in the labyrinth of secret apertures, concealed passages, skylights, manholes, trap doors, tunnels, cellars, and hidden exits and entrances. In fact, few policemen ever ventured into such dangerous quarters and never alone. Even harmless social workers and missionaries were not safe: a Protestant missionary who was

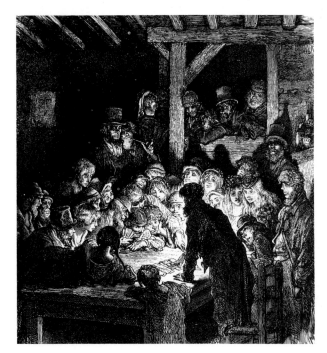

foolhardy enough to enter the kitchen of a lodginghouse in that dreadful part of Bloomsbury known as the Holy Land was set upon by a gang of women, who knocked him down and stripped him almost naked before their men folk dragged him outside, stuffed his mouth with mustard, and plunged him headfirst into a water butt.

The brutal behavior of the denizens of these rookeries seemed on occasion scarcely human: at Willenhall in Staffordshire in 1849 four men were tried for helping one another to rape a girl before a crowd of men, women, and children who had gathered to watch and to encourage the rapists to further cruelties. Murders were so common that Edwin Chadwick was driven to conclude that eleven thousand people died every year from acts of violence.

The penal system was as ill equipped to deal with this violence as it was to bring under control an underworld so vast and active that in 1867 in London alone, according to "reliable police statistics," there were no less than one hundred thousand persons who lived by plunder and did not know where their day's food was to come from when they got up in the morning.

The Victorian prison system certainly did nothing to reduce this appalling amount of crime, and many of its critics contested that it actually contributed to the increase of crime. Well aware that eighteenth-century prisons had been schools of crime for young offenders, prison reformers had been much impressed by the penal systems in operation in America, where convicts were forbidden to talk to one another and kept confined in separate cells. In England reforms had been slow to come, since the country had for generations found a convenient way of ridding itself of its hardened criminals by transporting to the colonies those who were allowed to escape hanging. But America had ceased to be a convenient dump-

There is a certain similarity between Gustave Doré's famous drawings of Dante's hell and the mordant views of the London underworld that he executed for Blanchard Jerrold's book London: a Pilgrimage. *Left is a gaming table and, opposite, an opium den. Once people were in such an atmosphere, a policeman told Jerrold, "the best of them are lost. They cann't help it. Some will struggle for a long time; but unless they . . . get away, they are done for."*

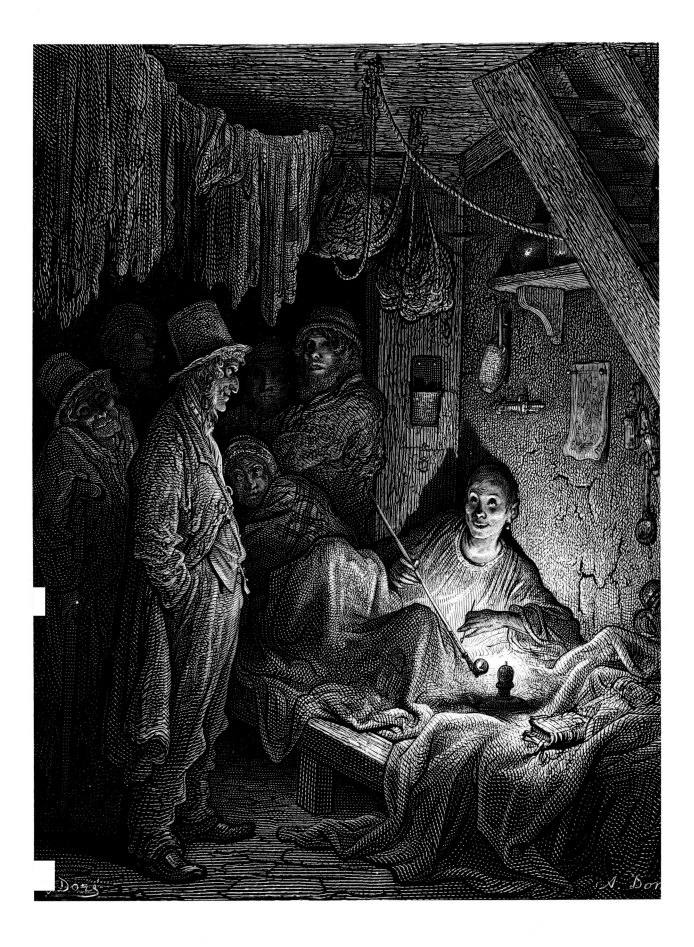

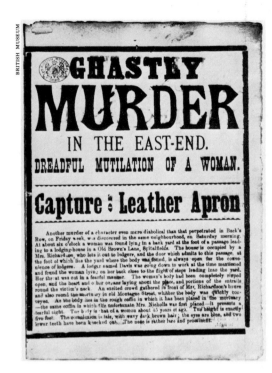

GHASTLY MURDER

IN THE EAST-END.
DREADFUL MUTILATION OF A WOMAN.

Capture of Leather Apron

Another murder of a character even more diabolical than that perpetrated in Buck's Row, on Friday week, was discovered in the same neighbourhood, on Saturday morning. At about six o'clock a woman was found lying in a back yard at the foot of a passage leading to a lodging-house in Old Brown's Lane, Spitalfields. The house is occupied by a Mrs. Richardson, who lets it out to lodgers, and the door which admits to this passage, at the foot of which lies the yard where the body was found, is always open for the convenience of lodgers. A lodger named Davis was going down to work at the time mentioned and found the woman lying on her back close to the flight of steps leading into the yard. Her throat was cut in a fearful manner. The woman's body had been completely ripped open, and the heart and other organs laying about the place, and portions of the entrails round the victim's neck. An excited crowd gathered in front of Mrs. Richardson's house and also round the mortuary in old Montague Street, whither the body was quickly conveyed. As the body lies in the rough coffin in which it has been placed in the mortuary —the same coffin in which the unfortunate Mrs. Nicholls was first placed—it presents a fearful sight. The body is that of a woman about 45 years of age. The height is exactly five feet. The complexion is fair, with wavy dark brown hair; the eyes are blue, and two lower teeth have been knocked out. The nose is rather large and prominent.

This broadside announced the horrors perpetrated by Jack the Ripper. The gentry below are studying wax heads of convicts.

ing ground after the War of Independence, and Australia's strong objections to being considered a penal colony subsequently brought an end to convict ships sailing there also. An extensive program of prison building had therefore become essential; and so it was that over fifty large prisons were built in England in the middle of the nineteenth century, many of them, like Reading Prison—to which Oscar Wilde was committed in 1895—constructed on the lines of medieval castles, combining "with the castellated . . . a collegiate appearance," and considered by students of architecture as among the best buildings of their respective counties.

One of the principal forerunners, a model for several other institutions in the provinces, was Pentonville, a huge penitentiary completed in London in 1842. It had 520 cells, each thirteen and a half feet long, seven and a half feet wide, and nine feet high, with a window overlooking the courtyard, a door leading out into the gallery, a stool, a table, a hammock, a gas burner, a water closet, a basin with hot and cold water, and a bell handle. It was, in fact, far more comfortable than most prison cells were to be a hundred years later. Nor was the food, though unappetizing, inadequate. It consisted of three quarters of a pint of cocoa and a large piece of bread for breakfast, soup or meat with potatoes and bread for dinner, and a pint of gruel with another big piece of bread for supper.

But the dreadful monotony and dreariness of the daily existence of convicts in Pentonville was insupportable. Work began at six o'clock in the morning and continued until seven at night with breaks only for meals, for brief periods of exercise, and for the daily service in the chapel, where each prisoner sat in a kind of box, unable to communicate with his neighbor, though his head was visible to the warder standing behind them. Indeed, so anxious were the authorities that the prisoners should not communicate with one another, or even recognize one another on the rare occasions when they came face to face, that they were all obliged to wear a mask of brown cloth, "the eyes alone of this individual appearing through the two holes cut in the front, and seeming almost like phosphoric lights shining through the sockets of a skull." Any attempt at communication was severely punished, the offender being placed in a refractory cell in total darkness, often for days on end.

Immediately on arrival in prison, the convict was made to feel that he was there to be punished not merely confined. Even the work to which he was put was a kind of punishment, often consisting of tasks as exhausting to perform as they were useless when completed. Common devices for keeping men occupied without endangering the livelihood of honest workers were the treadmill and the crank. Both could be employed for useful purposes, but it was rare that either was. The treadmill was an iron frame of steps around a revolving cylinder, divided into closed compartments in which prisoners, both male and female, were required to keep treading. "You see the men can get no firm tread like, from the steps always sinking away from under their feet," a warder explained, "and *that* makes it very tiring. Again the compartments are small, and the air becomes very hot, so that the heat at the end of a quarter of an hour renders it difficult to breathe."

The crank, a box of gravel fitted with a handle, which the prisoner had to turn through a prescribed number of revolutions, was equally exhausting. So was shot drill, a form of exercise in which the prisoners, standing nine feet apart and formed in rows, had to lift up cannon balls weighing twenty-four pounds each, carry them, drop them at the feet of their neighbors, and then return to their own places, repeating the process for seventy-five minutes. Picking bits of old rope to pieces, though painful for unhardened fingers, was not so exhausting but was equally pointless, since the work was continued long after the use of iron in the building of ships had made the resultant oakum largely unsalable. Unable to stand the silent drudgery and dreadful monotony, many prisoners came out of prison emotionally disturbed, as did the Shropshire pickpocket whose career has been described. Some became insane: during the first eight years of Pentonville's existence there were "upwards of ten times more lunatics than there should be according to the normal rate." Others committed suicide.

The inquest on a fifteen-year-old prisoner who had hanged himself in Birmingham Prison led to the exposure of fearful cruelties: of prisoners being systematically whipped, of them being set to perform impossible tasks at the crank and being

starved when they failed to complete them, of them being forced to endure long periods of solitary confinement in darkness and in strait jackets. A royal commission appointed in 1854 to inquire into such cruelties found equally painful examples at Leicester Prison. A subsequent royal commission, which held its hearings in 1879, discovered that convicts at Chatham were driven to satisfying their hunger on worms and that they threw themselves beneath the wheels of the railway wagons in the dock basins in order to escape from their misery and were flogged if they did not die, there being "no reason," the governor said, "why they should not be flogged, because they had only mutilated an arm or a leg."

By the 1870's, though, conditions at Chatham were exceptional. The system was slowly being reformed. A series of acts had created prison inspectors, removed prisons from the control of local authorities, segregated first offenders from the others, and introduced a system by which a prisoner might progress from a day involving six hours on the treadmill to a relatively comfortable life with letters and visitors. Nor, even in earlier years, had all prisons been nearly as bad as those whose squalor and cruelties were highlighted by official inquiries. Many houses of correction, in which short sentences were served, were run as humanely as their finances would allow. So were many local provincial jails. "We was all very happy and comfortable there, though we were kept rather short of victuals," a young navvy, who had been sentenced for horsewhipping a foreman, recalled of his two months in Lewes Gaol in the 1840's. "There they learnt me to spin mops, and it was there that I got hold of most of my scholarship. I learned to read from the turnkey— a very nice man. He come and stand by my cell door and help me to a word whenever I asked him, and a church parson used to preach us every morning of the week—and very good it was! It did me a deal of good going to prison, that time—it learned me to be a scholar and a better man."

Yet, even at the end of the century, there were many big prisons where the prisoners, though adequately clothed and fed and kept clean and warm, continued to endure an existence of unrelieved misery. At Dartmoor, an immense stone structure in Devon that had been built for prisoners of war during the Napoleonic Wars and had been used for convicts since 1850, a visitor was shocked as he walked along the "endless landings and corridors in the great cellular blocks."

I saw something of the 1,500 men who were then immured in Dartmoor. Their drab uniforms were plastered with broad arrows, their heads were closely shaven. . . . Not even a safety razor was allowed so that in addition to the stubble on their heads, their faces were covered with a sort of dirty moss, representing the growth of hair that a pair of clippers could not remove. . . . As they saw me coming each man turned to the nearest wall and put his face closely against it, remaining in this servile position until we had passed him. This was a strictly ordered procedure, to avoid assault or familiarity, the two great offences in prison conduct.

Although the gradual reduction in the amount of crime toward the end of the century could not be attributed to the reformatory effects of prisons, the new police were recognized as being important elements in its prevention. Due to the Englishman's distrust of any innovation that he thought might interfere with his traditional liberties, it was not until 1829 that Sir Robert Peel, the

home secretary, was able to persuade the House of Commons to pass the Metropolitan Police Act, which established a paid force of three thousand policemen in London. And even then they were widely resented, not only by radicals, who saw in a professional police force a possible instrument of tyranny, but also by the upper classes, who resented the police commissioner's refusal to provide employment for their ill-qualified nominees, and by magistrates, who thought that their own authority was in peril. Assaults on constables were extremely common, and the offenders were very lightly treated: a gang of men found guilty of attacking a group of constables, almost killing one and injuring eleven others, some of them severely, were merely bound over to keep the peace. As well as being resented policemen were poorly paid. A constable got no more than 19s. a week; an inspector less than £2. And a portion of this was deducted for their uniform. They wore blue tail coats with the number and letter of their division on the collar and top hats (until 1864, when they were provided with helmets), and as their only weapon, they carried short wooden batons.

It was not easy at first to find suitable recruits. Most of them were old soldiers, and as many as a third of the force were dismissed every year, mostly for drunkenness. Gradually, however, as

Convicts in Holloway Prison pick rope apart to make oakum while the men standing behind them work the treadmill.

pay and conditions of service improved, as the streets became quieter at night, and as trouble-makers found it more difficult to lead on a London mob to violence, people began to admit that the metropolitan police were not so unwelcome after all. Their numbers grew to nearly ten thousand, their efficiency increased at the same time, and their early nickname, blue devils, gave way to the almost affectionate "peeler" or "bobby," in commemoration of the man to whom they owed their existence.

Within a decade, in fact, their effectiveness in London had led to criminals seeking their prey elsewhere, and crime in provincial towns grew at an alarming rate. In Newcastle-on-Tyne it was calculated that one in twenty-seven of the population was a known bad character, and the proportion in other towns was scarcely more encouraging. So an act was passed permitting counties to raise and equip paid police forces; and those counties that took advantage of the act soon obliged others to follow their example. In 1856 a further act made it obligatory for all counties to raise and maintain a constabulary.

At first the provincial police were quite as unpopular as those in London. In Leeds when a notice appeared on a public house announcing, "No swaddy Irishmen or soldiers wanted here," several soldiers ran riot, attacking every passer-by

they came across. Yet a few months later, when fighting broke out between soldiers and police, it was reported that "the populace generally" sympathized with the soldiers. In time, though, the provincial police became as respected as the metropolitan police, and as in London, crime began to diminish. The police were not, of course, alone responsible. More important was the Victorians' rapidly growing social concern—a realization that the appalling conditions in which so many of the poor were required to live, those breeding grounds of crime in every city, could no longer be tolerated. There was another cause, too. At the beginning of the century it had often seemed that England might erupt in revolution. The militant activities of the Chartists posed a threat to the established order that no one could ignore. Yet by the middle of the century the danger had already passed. The last Chartist demonstration was no more than a demonstration. And to a large extent responsible for this was the growing influence of the non-conformist Christian sects and the simultaneous spread of those attributes commonly associated with the Victorian middle class.

When mothers went to jail, their children often went with them. Here they are exercising in the yard at Tothill Fields Prison.

CHAPTER X

FLESH AND THE SPIRIT

"Sexual indulgence before the age of twenty-five," ruled a medical textbook designed for the general public in the year of the queen's accession, "not only retards the development of the genital organs, but of the whole body, impairs the strength, injures the consitution and shortens life." By the end of the century the admonitory tone of such works as this had changed very little. Dr. William Acton, an authority more enlightened than most, whose influential *The Function and Disorders of the Reproductive Organs . . .* remained in print long after his death in 1875, warned his readers that masturbation, that "most vicious" form of incontinence, led to its practitioners becoming enfeebled in body and mind and "careless in dress and uncleanly in person"; creeping about alone, shunning the society of others, with sunken eye, damp, cold hands, and sallow complexion covered with spots; in danger of sinking finally into the state of "a drivelling idiot." This was a problem peculiarly male, since "the majority of women (happily for them)" were "not very much troubled with sexual feeling of any kind."

In polite society sex was just not discussed;

BY COURTESY OF CHRISTIE'S LTD., LONDON

In his painting The Doubt: "Can These Dry Bones Live?" *H. A. Bowler touched on three pervasive Victorian themes—death, religion, and idealized women. The woman above is rendering her virtue suspect by smoking a cigarette.*

and in the nursery any innocent questions were hastily brushed aside or evasively answered in terms of gooseberry bushes, storks, and doctors' bags. Sex was not only no fit subject for conversation; it was no proper theme for art. Royal Academy nudes could be sentimental and romantic; they must never be licentious. Sex, in fact, was best left hidden. It was a scourge, and by earnest endeavor a man could resist its dangerous temptations. Marriage offered a release from its toils; but as Acton warned, childbearing was almost a necessity in marriage, for rarely without a "fertile married life" could "excesses" be satisfactorily avoided "and sensual feelings in the man gradually sobered down."

In revolt against this middle-class morality, thousands of men left home from time to time in search of sexual excitement elsewhere. The number of prostitutes in England was known to be immense. W. T. Stead, who exposed in the *Pall Mall Gazette* the scandalous trade in the bodies of young children, estimated that in 1885 there were as many as sixty thousand prostitutes in London. Twenty years before, Bracebridge Hemyng estimated there were even more, excluding part-time prostitutes known as dolly mops and courtesans, kept in apartments that were visited by their gentlemen as opportunity permitted. Other gentlemen preferred the variety provided by the well-appointed brothels around St. James's and Curzon Street; by the

For the middle classes Sunday meant church, and church, of course, meant the Church of England. Here, dressed in their best clothes, members of a country congregation converge for services.

smart night-houses in Haymarket, like Kate Hamilton's, where well-dressed girls were admitted for inspection by the male patrons of the establishment; or on the promenade at the back of the royal circle of the Empire Theatre, where the more expensive prostitutes offered themselves with smiles and nods as they walked up and down between the velvet-covered couches. And for those who could not so easily leave home at night there were also plenty of girls to be found at all hours of the day around Windmill Street, where they had comfortable rooms on the upper floors; in the Strand, where there were numerous houses of accommodation; in Covent Garden, where several coffee houses had rooms to let for the afternoon; in Burlington Arcade, where a girl would nod the way into one of the shops and lead her customer up the stairs behind the counter; and in Rotten Row, where "pretty horse-breakers," working in partnership with the willing proprietors of livery stables,

rode about in fetching riding habits and coquettish little boots with military heels.

Most of the girls were young. Many were under thirteen, which was, until 1885, when it was raised to sixteen, the age of consent. Some were under ten. And, as Stead proclaimed, gentlemen paid large sums of money for these little virgins.

Maids as you call them—fresh girls as we know them in the trade—are constantly in request [a former brothel-keeper confessed to Stead]. A keeper who knows his business has his eye open in all directions. His stock of girls is constantly getting used up, and needs replenishing, and he has to be on the alert for likely "marks" to keep up the reputation of his house. The getting of fresh girls takes time, but it is simple and easy enough when once you are in it. I have gone and courted girls in the country under all kinds of disguises, occasionally assuming the dress of a parson, and made them believe I intended to marry them, and so got them in my power to please a good customer. . . . After courting my girl for a time, I propose to bring her to London to see the sights. I bring her up, take her here and there, giving her plenty to eat and drink—especially drink . . . I contrive it so that she loses her last train . . . I offer her nice lodgings for the night. . . . My client gets his maid. . . .

Another very simple mode of supplying maids is breeding them. Many women who are on the streets have female children. They are worth keeping . . . I know a couple of very fine little girls now who will be sold before long. They are bred and trained for the life. They must take the first step sometime, and it is bad business not to make as much out of that as possible. Drunken parents often sell their children to brothel-keepers. In the East-end you can always pick up as many fresh girls as you want.

The insatiable middle-class author of *My Secret Life* claimed to have bought one of these little virgins for £200; but his pleasures were usually far less expensive than this, though he complained toward the end of the century that the cost of women, like the cost of everything else, was going up all the time. In his youth, he said, "a sovereign would get any woman, and ten shillings as nice a one as you needed. Two good furnished rooms near the Clubs could be had by women for from fifteen to twenty shillings per week. . . . I got quite nice girls at from five to ten shillings a poke, and had several in their own rooms, but sometimes paying half-a-crown extra for a room elsewhere. [One of these girls] was young, handsome, well made, and in the Haymarket would now get anything from one to five pounds; yet I had her several times for three or four shillings a time."

Although Dostoevski said that in the Haymarket area whores gathered "in their thousands" and Taine complained that "every hundred steps in the Strand he was jostled by twenty harlots," condemnations of the supposedly high-minded Victorians as a race of hypocrites are misleading and unfair. Admittedly the seduction of maidservants by the sons or masters of the house was by no means uncommon—indeed, the servants frequently expected it, encouraged it, and accepted that they would be blamed and dismissed if caught. Acton went further and maintained that vast numbers of men, married and single, made a "sport and a habit" out of seducing any pretty, available working-class girl; and since birth control was rarely practiced before the 1870's, pregnancy often resulted.

Yet the average middle-class Victorian was genuinely shocked by sexual promiscuity and sincerely convinced that a better, more fulfilled and enjoyable life could be lived in the earnest pursuit of wealth and of a respected place in society than in the manifestly transient and probably deleterious pleasures of sex. In this belief he was strengthened and comforted by his religious faith.

Christianity was of profound importance to him. Its precepts permeated his nursery. At his public school he was told, as Dr. Arnold's pupils were told at Rugby, that "religious and moral principles" were above all required of him: they were even more important than "gentlemanly conduct," which was itself to be more highly regarded than intellectual ability. In his adult life he was conscious always that the probity of his conduct was God's concern: straight dealing would be rewarded, dishonesty punished in an afterlife. There were, of course, men like Lord Melbourne who were reluctant to let "religion interfere with private life," but they were in the minority. Most men let their lives be ruled by it. Prayers began the schoolboys' day as they did the business of Parliament. Clerks were called in for Bible reading before sitting down at their ledgers. Servants entered the drawing room or library to pray with their master and to listen to him read a sermon.

There were Roman Catholics, Quakers, high Anglicans and low, and nonconformists of all kinds. But the pervasive doctrine was one of salvation by works, a kind of broad evangelicalism that laid such stress on the Bible that copies of the sacred text were placed on reading stands in main-line railway stations. Evangelicalism accepted without question that there was a heaven and a hell and that this earth was a testing ground. It taught men to believe that pleasure in itself was an unworthy pursuit and that contentment was reached through self-improvement.

Outward observance was no less important than inner faith. The masses, as Charles Booth discovered, did not go to church in the morning, nor did "any very large numbers" go in the evening. But middle-class attendance was *de rigueur*. In 1851 a census of church attendance showed that well over seven million out of a

total population in England and Wales of under eighteen million attended some place of worship on one day, a proportion ten times as great as it was to be a hundred years later. Many commentators were shocked that the proportion in 1851 was not higher than it was—the Scots did better by seven per cent than the English and Welsh—but the respectable middle classes were not held responsible. To be sure, by the end of the century middle-class church attendance was dropping, but during most of the queen's reign churches and chapels were full.

It could not be pretended, though, that the entire congregation derived either pleasure or profit from attendance. "My back still aches in memory of those long services," a writer recalled of his middle-class childhood in the 1870's. "Nothing was spared us—the whole of the 'Dearly Beloved,' never an ommission of the Litany, always the full ante-Communion Service, involving a sermon of unbelievable length. The seats and kneeling boards were constructed for grown-ups (and none too comfortable for them), and a child had the greatest difficulty in keeping an upright kneeling position all through the long intoned Litany." For a child the sermons were the most dreaded part of the service. Many a country squire followed the example of the prince of Wales at Sandringham: he took a good, hard look at his watch, then fixed his eyes upon the parson and made clear his displeasure if the sermon lasted for more than ten minutes. But in larger churches, and in nonconformist chapels, such checks on the preacher were not so easily effected. Methodist preachers rarely spoke for less than an hour, and the Reverend C. H. Spurgeon addressed his congregations for a far longer period than this. And although children were worn out by Spurgeon's addresses, their elders flocked to hear him by the thousands. When he preached at the South London Baptist Tabernacle every one of the five thousand seats was filled. He spoke "with a wonderful assurance" from a long balcony, walking up and down continually, "addressing first one

In this unusually daring music-hall poster, a soubrette toasts her admirers, among them, chewing on his cigar, the prince of Wales.

117

portion and then another of his vast congregation," and commanding the attention of his listeners for hours on end. When his own chapel proved too small for him, Spurgeon hired the premises of the Surrey Music Hall Company and preached there until one Sunday "a cry of fire being raised, there was a rush for the doors, seven people being killed, and fifty injured. Spurgeon remained calm."

Having been to church, most families returned home; for as a writer in *Household Words* observed in 1853, "a Sunday holiday is looked upon as a heinous sin by so many respectable people that it cannot be indulged in with impunity." When bands were given permission to play in the new public parks in Manchester and Salford in 1856, "the opposition on the part of the Sabbatarian public was so strongly expressed that the experiment was soon abandoned."

To-day is a Sunday [a Swiss tourist who had come to England for the Great Exhibition recorded gloomily in 1851] and I . . . walked down Cheapside which is quite a long street. I would have liked to have gone into a coffee-house for a glass of ale or claret but all the shops were hermetically sealed. . . . Even the front door of my own hotel was locked and only if one knew the secret could one turn the right knob and effect an entry. Otherwise there would be nothing for it but to ring the bell. On returning to my hotel I asked for my bill as I have been accustomed to settle my account every day. But the innkeeper politely asked me to wait until Monday. . . . I got into an argument with a young lady who strongly criticised Parliament for allowing trains, omnibuses and cabs to run on Sundays. She explained that her own pious family always observed the Sabbath strictly. To illustrate this she explained that since her papa's funeral had taken place on a Sunday . . . his hearse had been drawn by hired horses and not by the family horses.

In *Little Dorrit* Dickens described how a Sunday in London appeared to Arthur Clennam, who, newly arrived from Marseilles, sat in the window of a coffee house (one, at least, was open) on Ludgate Hill.

It was a Sunday evening in London, gloomy, close and stale. Maddening church bells of all degrees of dissonance, sharp and flat, cracked and clear, fast and slow, made the brick-and-mortar echoes hideous. . . . In every thoroughfare, up almost every alley, and down almost every turning, some doleful bell was throbbing. . . . Everything was bolted and barred that could by possibility furnish relief to an overworked people. . . . Nothing to see but streets, streets, streets. Nothing for the spent toiler to do. . . . [The peal of the nearest church bell] revived a long train of miserable Sundays. . . . There was the dreary Sunday of his childhood, when he sat with his hands before him, scared out of his senses by a horrible tract which commenced business with the poor child by asking him in its title, why he was going to Perdition? . . . There was the interminable Sunday of his nonage; when his mother . . . would sit all day behind a Bible. . . . There was the resentful Sunday of a little later, when he sat glowering and glooming through the tardy length of the day, with a sullen sense of injury in his heart, and no more real knowledge of the beneficent history of the New Testament than if he had been bred among idolaters.

If a Sunday in London was tedious, it was even more so in provincial cities, and compared with Edinburgh, a London sabbath, in Taine's opinion, was "positively agreeable." Neither in Scotland nor in England were games played; places of amusement were shut; in the country field sports were abandoned for the day. Behind closed doors the families of the city settled down after church to their Sunday occupations. In many families most of the amusements permitted on other days were forbidden. Even reading was subject to restraint.

Much of what was published was banned from respectable homes in any case. The "penny dreadfuls," the "shilling shockers," and the cheap weekly magazines were all outlawed as a matter of course. So were Sunday newspapers that, like *Reynolds's Weekly*, reported the most scandalous

The themes of Dissipation (left), Industry (right), and Penitence (center) ennoble this 1857 composite photograph Two Ways of Life. *The queen admired it and gave a copy to Prince Albert.*

gossip and gave prominence to detailed police reports. And novels that would have been considered unobjectionable on a weekday were also often banned on Sundays, though great care was taken by every reputable, popular writer to insure that no offense was given to the susceptibilities of his audience. Dickens, for instance, the most popular novelist of his day, was always aware that he was writing for a family audience; and although he hinted at terrible things, he declined to pull back the veil from the shocking truth. Worldly readers might well presume that Bill Sykes's Nancy was a whore and might well imagine what Quilp was really up to when he jumped into Little Nell's bed and blazed away in it with his cigar; but Dickens considered it no part of his duty as an author to tell them. Other writers were equally discreet, or if they were not, their publishers declined to publish what they had written or altered offending words. When George Eliot described Mrs. Moss in *The Mill on the Floss* as "a patient, loosely-hung, child-producing woman," her publisher protested that the words were rather overexplicit; and on the book's appearance in 1860, Mrs. Moss was introduced as "a patient, prolific, loving-hearted woman." Thomas Hardy's publisher was equally anxious to preserve his own reputation and asked that "lewd" become "gross"; "loose," "wicked"; and "amorous," "sentimental." Even thus diluted some of Hardy's novels were considered too daring for the readership of the magazines in which they were serialized: readers of *Tess of the d'Urbervilles* in the *Graphic* were told that Angel Clare took the milkmaid across the flooded stream in a wheelbarrow, not in his strong arms.

Yet on a Sunday even the most inoffensive novels, which could by no stretch of a prurient imagination be considered as straying toward the bounds of impropriety, were left unopened in the stricter middle-class homes. Sunday was the day for improving works of biography and history, for religious tracts and periodicals, and above all for the Bible and sermons. The amount of religious literature published was enormous. There were numerous religious family papers, such as *Christian World, Leisure Hour,* and *Christian Herald;* the total circulation of monthly periodicals of a religious nature published in London in 1864 was almost two million. The number of new re-

ligious books published each year was equally impressive. According to the *Publisher's Circular* of 1870 new books on religious subjects far outstripped publications on any other subject. "Juvenile works and tales" came a poor second, and these included many more books of a religious nature. Books of sermons sold particularly well, and many a poor clergyman made far more out of publishing his sermons than he received as his stipend.

The picture of a middle-class family sitting in gloomy silence, reading sermons and longing for Sunday to be over, does not, however, truly reflect the whole Victorian middle class. There were families, of course, like the Ruskins, who turned their pictures to the wall on Sundays and always ate cold meals so that the servants had time to worship and study as they did themselves. Societies like that founded for Promoting the External Observance of the Lord's Day and for the Suppression of Public Lewdness did have wide influence. Yet the Victorians were not a generally gloomy people. Sunday was the Lord's Day. But it was also a day of rest, and not every child was bored. One middle-class Victorian child remembered Sunday as being:

a day when papa was at home. We never saw him in the week. He went to his office very early and we were all in bed when he got home. But on Sundays in the afternoons we were all together round the fire. We had tea in the dining-room. There were four different kinds of jam. After tea he read to us and gave us toffees. I remember how carefully we unwrapped the paper so as not to make a noise. We were not allowed to play ordinary games on Sundays. But we could bring our dolls downstairs; and have them in the drawing-room. We used to take it in turns to sit on his knee; and play with his watch which he kept on a gold chain in his waistcoat pocket. It had a gold flap that opened up at the back and you could pull this back and see the works inside, and he used to tell us stories about the little people who lived inside and peeped out from behind the wheels but always nipped away before we could catch a glimpse of them. Before going upstairs we read to ourselves when we were old enough. Papa's favourite author was George Eliot. Our friends told us that they had to read books about church and deathbeds but we could have our magazines, the *Monthly Packet* and *Little Folks.* Papa would light his cigar and stop reading from time to time to look at us through the smoke. I can smell the smoke now and see the look in his eyes as I

Augustus L. Egg's dramatic bit of moral instruction shows a faithless wife sobbing on the floor while her husband looks on grimly and the children's house of cards collapses.

smiled at him. . . . On Sunday nights he came to watch us have our bath.

It was this child's nurse's motto that cleanliness came next to godliness. Most other middle-class children were brought up to believe this too. Foreigners certainly considered the English to be almost neurotically concerned with keeping clean. "The English," Heinrich von Treitschke once told a class of German students, "think soap is civilisation." A visitor at any large city in early Victorian England would have found little evidence for this belief: most of the streets were still unpaved, and few of the houses in the poorer quarters had either a water tap or any form of drainage. In Birmingham in the 1840's only one house in five had any kind of water supply, in Newcastle only one in twelve, and in other towns where the proportion was higher the water was frequently either inadequate or impure. In many places the poor had to walk long distances to find any water that was fit to drink and conse-

quently made do with polluted river water for washing, if, indeed, they could be bothered to fetch water at all for so inessential a purpose. Outside privies, built over cesspits or wet middens and shared by several families, were common until the very end of the century.

Such insanitary conditions took an appalling toll of life. Most mothers were accustomed to the idea that to have two surviving children they would have to undergo five or six births. In Liverpool the expectation of life among laborers was only fifteen years, in Manchester seventeen, and in Leeds nineteen. In country districts it was rather higher: in Cornwall a farm worker could expect to live to be twenty-eight and in Wiltshire, thirty-three. Living in more sanitary surroundings and eating better food, farmers could look forward to a longer life—forty-eight years in Wiltshire; and the gentry lived longer still: a Somersetshire landowner could expect to live to be fifty-five. But even the richest and most privileged were not immune. Prince Albert died at the age of forty-two after succumbing to typhoid fever at Windsor Castle, where fifty overflowing cesspits were found beneath the floors. The prince of Wales almost died of the same disease after a visit to Londesborough Lodge, whose foul drains killed his fellow guest Lord Chesterfield. At another country mansion footmen frequently complained of sore throats after using the pantry sink; but it was not until the weight of a carriage caused the courtyard outside to give way, revealing a forgotten cesspool, that the reason for the footmen's recurring malady was discovered. Some of the smartest and most expensive districts in London were built over sewers from which thousands of rats crawled up every night in search of food; and reports of rats being found in the cots of well-to-do children were not at all uncommon.

But after generations of neglect and ignorance the most outrageous conditions were overcome. It was realized that bad drains were not "rather a joke," as Lady Georgiana Russell said they were in early Victorian England, when so many people of all classes died of mysterious fevers. And due to the persistence of such outspoken critics as Edwin Chadwick, and the support given to the reformers by influential laymen, like Charles Kingsley, the country was made to realize the closeness of the connection between sanitation and ill health. By 1875 Parliament had passed the vitally important Third Public Health Act, which provided local authorities with extensive powers to maintain water and sewage systems, to clean the streets, to deal with infections, to appoint medical officers of health, in fact, to lay the foundations of a new form of social service.

Such an act had long been needed. There had been repeated outbreaks of cholera throughout the century, the highest number of deaths being recorded in the towns with the worst drainage systems and water supplies. There had also been periodic outbreaks of smallpox, which killed twenty-three thousand people in 1871. Typhoid fever, scarlet fever, diphtheria, pyemia, measles,

and ptomaine poisoning had all claimed numerous victims every year. But after the act of 1875 the nation's health began to improve. The people's fear of vaccination gradually disappeared, disinfectants and prophylactics came into general use, and hospitals became associated with cure rather than death.

In the last two decades of the century many new hospitals were built and many more remodeled on the lines of St. Thomas's Hospital, which was entirely reconstructed in accordance with Florence Nightingale's insistence on the importance of the free circulation of air and the isolation of infectious patients. It was at St. Thomas's that Miss Nightingale had started her influential nurse's school in 1860, a time when the few female nurses that there were had a reputation for drunkenness and slovenly lubricity. Within forty years there were sixty-four thousand trained nurses in the country, and the profession of nurs-

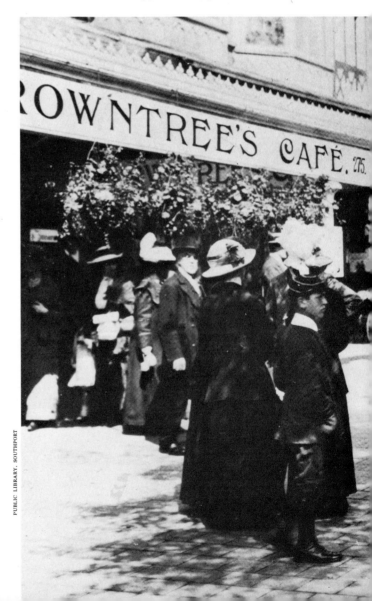

Well-dressed ladies stop to chat on the busy, pleasant thoroughfare Lord Street in Southport at the turn of the century.

ing had been transformed. So had the medical profession as a whole. Anesthetics developed rapidly after their pioneering use by William T. G. Morton in the United States and Sir James Simpson in England; and antiseptic surgery was standard practice soon after Joseph Lister introduced carbolic acid into the operating theatre.

Lord Willoughby de Broke believed that of all nineteenth-century inventions it was anesthetics that had contributed most to the improved quality of life in late Victorian England. But whatever credit was given to the enormous variety of inventions, to those individual reformers who had fought injustice, ignorance, and intolerance, or to those social and economic forces that had swept away the past, there was no doubt that for the great mass of people the quality of life *had* improved in almost every material way since the Victorians had first become aware of their own identity.

Went to my club [a London merchant recorded in his diary on January 23, 1901, after news had come from Osborne House that the old queen had died at half past six the evening before]. The streets were crowded as usual. But there seemed an unusual hush over the traffic and the people I passed looked at me as though I were in need of their sympathy, as though we have shared a loss in the family—as, I suppose, in a way we have. I fell to thinking of the day I had come down to London from the north, and the first time I had gone to the club where I have been having lunch on and off now for the best part of forty years and of all the changes I have seen. Not just in the way we live but in the way we think about things. . . . I don't suppose another forty years in the whole history of England has seen so many changes. . . . People generally are more content—more placid too perhaps. We have much to be thankful for, though much to regret. . . . You don't see the poverty now; but you don't see the variety either. What a great time to have lived through! . . . But I wonder what our sons and grandsons will make of it all. It will be like reading about another world.

124   *There were celebrations throughout the empire during the queen's Diamond Jubilee year of 1897. A. C. Gow's*

painting shows the monarch arriving at St. Paul's amid clouds of magnificently caparisoned men and horses. 125

Staff for this Book

Editor Joseph J. Thorndike
Managing Editor Beverley Hilowitz
Art Director Elaine Golt Gongora
Picture Editor Mary Jenkins
Assistant Picture Editor Ellen F. Zeifer
Copy Editor Joan Wilkinson
Assistant Editors Sandra J. Wilmot
 Susan E. Green
European Bureau Gertrudis Feliu, *Chief*
London Correspondent Christine Sutherland
AMERICAN HERITAGE PUBLISHING CO., INC.
President and Publisher Paul Gottlieb
General Manager, Book Division Kenneth W. Leish
Editorial Art Director Murray Belsky

Acknowledgments

In the preparation of this book, the editors and author have enjoyed the help of many institutions and individuals. We would like particularly to thank the following:

The Bettmann Archive, New York
Phyllis Grygalin, Time-Life Picture Agency, New York
Helen Hettinger, The English-Speaking Union, New York
Bob Jackson, Culver Pictures, New York
Peter Jackson, London
Martha Jenks, George Eastman House, Rochester, New York
May Ellen MacNamara, Gernsheim Collection, University of Texas, Austin
Mansell Collection, London
Radio Times Hulton Picture Library, London
Gordon Winter, London

Permissions

The excerpts on the pages listed below have been reprinted from the following books with the kind permission of their publishers:

Pages 5, 7, 19–20, 57: *The Glitter and The Gold,* by Consuela Vanderbilt Balsan. New York, Harper & Row, 1952.
Page 14: *Recollections of Three Reigns,* by Sir Frederic Ponsonby. New York, E.P. Dutton & Co., Inc., 1952.
Page 19: *From Hall-Boy to House-Steward,* by William Lanceley. London, Edward Arnold Publishers, Ltd., 1925.
Pages 25–26: *The Carlyles at Home,* by Thea Holme. New York, Oxford University Press, 1965.
Pages 55, 58, 63: *Lark Rise,* by Flora Thompson. New York, Oxford University Press, 1939.

FRONT COVER: *Detail from "The Railway Station" by William Powell Frith. University of London, Royal Holloway College.*
CONTENTS PAGE: *A family of six with cycles. Gernsheim Collection, University of Texas, Austin.*

Bibliography

The best recent surveys of Victorian society are two volumes in The History of British Society series, edited by E. J. Hobsbawn:
Best, Geoffrey. *Mid-Victorian Britain.* London, Weidenfeld & Nicolson, 1971.
Harrison, J.F.C. *The Early Victorians, 1832–1851.* London, Weidenfeld & Nicolson, 1971.

For a good overall view of the period:
Ensor, R.C.K. *England, 1870–1914.* Harlow, Essex, Longmans Publishing Group, Ltd., 1950.
Mitchell, R.J. and Leys, M.D.R. *A History of the English People.* Harlow, Essex, Longmans Publishing Group, Ltd., 1950.
Perry, George and Mason, Nicholas. *The Victorians, A World Built to Last.* New York, Viking Press, 1974.
Reader, W.J. *Victorian England.* London, Batsford Publishers, Ltd., 1964.

Woodward, Sir Llewellyn. *The Age of Reform.* London, Oxford University Press, 1962.
Young, G.M. *Portrait of an Age: Victorian England.* London, Oxford University Press, paperback edition, 1973.
Young, G.M., ed. *Early Victorian England.* 2 vols. London, Oxford University Press, 1934.

On Victorian culture and society:
Altick, Richard D. *Victorian People and Ideas.* New York, Norton Publishing Co., 1974.
Black, Eugene C., ed. *Victorian Society and Culture.* New York, Harper & Row, 1973.
Booth, Charles. *Charles Booth's London,* edited by Albert Fried and Richard Elman. London, Hutchinson Publishers Ltd., 1969.
Mayhew, Henry. *London Labour and the London Poor (1851–1862),* edited by Peter Quennell. London, William Kimber, 1950–51.

Pike, E. Royston. *Human Documents of the Age of the Forsytes.* London, Allen & Unwin, 1969.

More specific works are the following:
Briggs, Asa. *Victorian Cities.* London, Odhams Publishers, 1963. New York, Harper & Row paperback edition, 1970.
Abel-Smith, Brian and Robert Pinker. *The Hospitals, 1800–1949: a study in social administration in England and Wales.* Cambridge, Mass., Harvard University Press, 1964.
Burnett, John. *Useful Toil: Autobiographies of British Working Class People, 1820–1920.* Bloomington, Indiana, Indiana University Press, 1974.
Chesney, Kellow. *The Anti-Society: An Account of the Victorian Underworld.* London, Penguin Books, Ltd., 1972.
Hibbert, Christopher. *The Roots of Evil: A Social History of Crime and Punishment.* Boston, Little, Brown, 1963.

Laver, James. *Victoriana.* New York, Hawthorn Books, Inc. 1967.
Lochhead, Marion. *The Victorian Household.* London, John Murray, Publisher, 1964.
Marcus, Stephen. *The Other Victorians.* London, Weidenfeld & Nicolson, 1966.
Perkin, Harold. *The Origins of Modern English Society 1780–1880.* also, *The Victorian City: Images and Realities,* edited by H.J. Dyos and Michael Wolf. London, Routledge & Kegan Paul, 1973.
Ranhofer, Charles. *The Epicurean.* New York, Dover, 1971.
Reeve, F.A. *Victorian and Edwardian Cambridge.* London, B.T. Batsford Ltd., 1971.
Winter, Gordon. *A Country Camera, 1844–1914.* London, Country Life Ltd., 1966.

INDEX

Numbers in boldface type refer to illustrations.

A

Acton, Dr. William, 113, 115
Adelphi Hotel, London, 87
Advertising, **30–31**
Africa, 32
Agar, criminal, 105–6
Agnes Grey (Brontë), 45
Agriculture, **54**, 55, 56, **57**, 58–59, 62–64, 67
Aire River, 69
Albert, prince consort, 14, 82, 119, 122
Albert Edward, prince of Wales, 13, 57, 117, **117**, 122
Althorp, 20
Alton, Hampshire, 96, **97**
America, 64, 87, 106, 108
Anderson, Elizabeth Garrett, 38
Andover, Hampshire, 56
Anglican Church. *See* Church of England
Animals, 45, 46, **90**, 96–97
  See also Hunting
Arnold, Thomas, 47, 115
Artisans, 72, 90
Astley's Theatre, London, 93
Atlantic cable, 34
Australia, 64, 108

B

Badminton, Wiltshire, **12–13**
Ball on Shipboard (Tissot), **11**
Balmoral Castle, Aberdeen, Scotland, 14
Barnard Castle, Durham, **15**
Barnardo, Dr., orphanage, 52, **53**
Barnsley, Yorkshire, 75
Barnum and Bailey Circus, 90, **91**
Barraud, William and Henry, painting by, **12–13**
Bath, marchioness of, 19
Bath, Somersetshire, 23
Beale, Dorothea, 48
Bear Wood, 20–21
Beaufort, Henry, seventh duke of, **12–13**
Bedford, duchess of, 9–10
Bedford, duke of, 5–6
Bedford Hotel, London, 87
Bedfordshire, 6
Beeton, Isabella, 27
Beeton's Book of Household Management, 27
Belvoir Castle, 9
Berkshire, 6
Bernhardt, Sarah, 10
Besant, Sir Walter, 29
Bible, 115, 119
Binny, John, 104, 105
Birmingham, England, 67, 72, 84, 86, 106, 121
Birmingham Prison, 109
Blackfriars Bridewell, London, 104
Blackwell, Elizabeth, 38
Blanc, Mont, **96**
Bleak House (Dickens), 80
Blenheim Palace, Oxfordshire, 5, 6–7
Blessington, countess of, 87
Bloomer, Amelia Jenks, 12
Booth, Charles, 69–70, 72, 115
Boulter's Lock, Maidenhead, **94**, 95
Bourne, Mrs. Addley, 38
Bowes, John, 15
Bowler, H. A., painting by, **112**, 113
Bowler, John, 14
Bradford, Yorkshire, 22, 69
Braham, John, 41
Brighton, East Sussex, 86, 98
Bristol, Gloucestershire, 90, **91**
Brontë, Anne, 45
Broughton Castle, 20
Brunel, Isambard Kingdom, **34**, 86
Bryanston, Dorsetshire, 14
Buccleuch, duke of, 5, 6
Buckingham, duke of, 15
Buckingham Palace, London, 21
Buckinghamshire, 6
Burghley, William Cecil, 1st baron, 55
Buss, Frances Mary, 48
Bute, third marquis of, 5, 14
Butler, Samuel, 47

C

Cambridge University, 33, 34, 48, **49**, 50, 100
Canterbury, archbishopric of, 58
Canterbury, Kent, 81
Cardiff Castle, 14
Cardigan, earl of, 15
Carlisle, countess of, 58
Carlton Hotel, London, 87
Carlyle, Jane, 25–26, 27, 38
Carlyle, Thomas, 25–26, 27
Carroll, Lewis, 41
  Photograph by, **40**
Carte, Richard D'Oyly, 87
Chadwick, Edwin, 106, 122
Chartists, 16, 105, 111
Chatham Prison, 109
Chatsworth, Derbyshire, 83
Cheltenham Ladies' College, 48
Chesterfield, Lord, 122
Children, 34–35, 38, **40**, 41–52, **53**, 60–61, 74–76, 98, 113
Christian, prince of Schleswig-Holstein, 14
Christian Herald, newspaper, 120
Christian World, newspaper, 120
Christianity, 115
  See also Church of England; Religion
Church of England, 48, 58, **114**, 115
Churchill, Lord Randolph, 55
Clarendon, fourth earl of, 47
Clive, Reverend Archer, 34
Clothing, 7, 10–14, 17, 23, 32, 38, **39**, **59**, 90, 98
Cobden, Richard, 15
Coburg (Vic) Theatre, London, 95
Commons, House of, 16, 56, 110
Cornwall, **60–61**, **64–65**, 121
Cosmetics, 10, 32
Cotton, George Edward Lynch, 47
Covent Garden Theatre, London, 93, 114
Cowes, Isle of Wight, **11**
Cremorne, King's Road, Chelsea, 38
Crime, **102**, 103–11, **111**, 113–15
Crimea, 35
Crystal Palace, Hyde Park, London, 33
Crystal Palace, Sydenham, 38
Cubitt, Thomas, 14
Curtis family, 96, **97**

D

Daisy Chain (Yonge), 42
Dana, Richard Henry, 20
Dancing, 32, 38, 90
Dante Alighieri, 106
Dartmoor Prison, Princeton, Devonshire, 109–10
Derby Day (Frith), **92–93**, 99
Derbyshire, **72**, 104
Devonshire, 109
Devonshire, duke of, 5
Diamond Jubilee, 5, **124–25**
Diary of a Nobody (Grossmith), 79–80
Dickens, Charles, 26–27, 35, **35**, 38, 46, 50–51, 80, 81, 89, 103, 118, 120
Dickens, John, 26–27
Disease, 35, 121–22
Disraeli, Benjamin, 5
Dodd, William, 74
Dombey and Son (Dickens), 46, 85–86
Don't: A Manual of Mistakes and Improprieties more or less prevalent in Conduct and Speech, 30
Doré, Gustave, 79, 103, 106
  Engravings by, **78**, **102**, **106**, **107**
Dostoevski, Fëdor, 115
Doubt, The: "Can These Dry Bones Live?" (Bowler), **112**, 113
Dover, Kent, 105
Doyle, Richard, 98
Dudley, Worcestershire, 76
Durham, bishopric of, 58
Durham, University of, 48
Dyott, General William, 56

E

Eaton Hall, Cheshire, 14, 20, 41, 57
Edinburgh, Scotland, 81, 119
Education, 41, **41**, 45, 46–52, 58–59
Edward VII, king. *See* Albert Edward, prince of Wales
Egg, Augustus L., painting by, **121**
Eliot, George, 34, 120
Ellis and Blackmore, solicitors, 80
Emerson, Ralph Waldo, 41
Empire Theatre, London, 114
Englishwoman's Domestic Magazine, 34
Epsom Downs, Surrey, 99, 104
Escoffier, Auguste, 87
Essex, 67
Etiquette, 29–32
Eton College, Buckinghamshire, 47, 82
Europe, 64
Euston Station, London, 84
Evans, Marian. *See* Eliot, George
Exeter Mail Coach, 81

F

Factories, 67–68, **68–69**, **72**, 73–74, 76
Factory acts, 74, 76, 90
Fairbairn, Sir William, 73
Fairs, 89–90
Family life, 34–35, 38–39, 41, 79–80
Far from the Madding Crowd (Hardy), 59, 62
Farnborough, Hampshire, 99
Fashion. *See* Clothing; Cosmetics
Field Lane Refuge, London, 73
Fielding, Henry, 56
Fisher, Major C. Hawkins, **59**
Folkestone, Kent, 105
Food and drink, 7–10, 17, 19–20, 21, 22, 23–24, 25, 26, 29, 30, 31, 33, 38, 39, 41–42, 43, **62**, 64, 70, 72, 73, 74, **74**, **75**, 76, 83, 84, 86–87, 89, 92, 93, 95, 96, 99, 104, 108
Forster, John, 38, 81
Fortnum and Mason's, London, 38
Fowey, Cornwall, **60–61**, 61
Framley Parsonage (Trollope), 58
France, 31, 100
Francis, John, 83
Frith, William Powell, 99
  Paintings by, **84–85**, **92–93**, 113
Functions and Disorders of the Reproductive Organs (Acton), 113

G

Galen, 48
Gambling, 96–97
Gaskell, Elizabeth Cleghorn, 58
Gentleman's House (Kerr), 20
Germany, 45
Gilbert, Sir William Schwenck, 98
Gladstone, William Ewart, 47, 55, 82
Glasgow, Scotland, 67, 68, 70
Golden Jubilee, 29
Gore House, Kensington, 87
Gott family, 73
Gow, A.C., painting by, **124–25**
Grace, W. G., 100
Great Britain, railway train, 82
Great Eastern, ship, 34
Great Exhibition of 1851, 24, **33**, 36–37, 105, 118
Great Landowners of Great Britain, 17
Great North Railway, 86
Great Western Railway, 34
Greenwich, London, 89
Gregory, Edward J., painting by, **94**, 95
Grossmith, George and Weedon, 79–80

H

Habits of Good Society, 30, 32
Hamilton, Lord Ernest, 57
Hamilton, Kate, 114
Hammersley, Mrs., 6
Hampshire, 83
Hansom, Joseph, 81
Hard Times (Dickens), 51
Hardy, Thomas, 59, 62, 120
Hare, Augustus, 42–45, 46

Harris, Betty, 75
Harrod's, London, 28, 38
Harrow School, London, 46, 47
Hastings, first marquis of, 15
Hatherton, Lord, 16
Haymarket, London, 10, 93, 114, 115
Heart of the Empire, **16–17**
Heenan, John C., 99
Helena Victoria, princess, 14
Hemyng, Bracebridge, 113
Highland Railway, 15
Hippocrates, 48
Holidays, 35, 38
Holloway Prison, 105, **110**
Holme, Thea, 25–26
Hotels, 86–87, **87**, 118
Household effects, **6**, 8, **9**, 24–25, **24–25**, 27, **29**, **33**, **39**, **44**, 63
Household Words, 118
Housing, 14, **15**, 20–21, 24, 43, 45, **55**, 63–64, 68–70, **70**, **71**, 72, 81, 86, 103, 106, 121
  See also Slums
Hudson, George, 83
Hughes, Taff, 103
Hughes, Thomas, 46–47
Hulmet, Lancashire, 52
Hunting, **12–13**, 56–57
Hurstmonceaux, East Sussex, 42
Huxley, Thomas H., 39
Hyde Park, London, **36–37**
Hygiene, **46**, 90, 98, 121

I

Ilfracombe, Devonshire, **50**
Illustrated Police News, illustrations from, **105**
Immigration, 68
India, 34, **88**, 89
Industrial Revolution, 25, 33
Industry, 55, **67**, 67–68, **68–69**, 70, **72**, 72–76, **76**, **77**, 85, 90
Inns. *See* Hotels
Ireland, 68, 100
Irving, Henry, 10, 79
Iwerne Minster, 14

J

Jack the Ripper, 108
Jeffries, Richard, 58
Jerrold, Blanchard, 106
Johnson, Samuel, 50
Jubilees, 5, 29, **124–25**

K

Kemble, Fanny, 9, 26
Kennington, London, 105
Kent, 62, 98
Kerr, Robert, 20
Kersal Moor, 92
Kersal Toll Bar, 73
Kilvert, Francis, 32, 46, 98
King's College, Cambridge, 48
Kingsley, Charles, 16, 39, 122

L

Labor, **18**, 19–27, 38–39, 52, 63–64, **64–65**, 66, 67–76, **77**, 83–84, 90, 103–4
Laguerre, Louis, 5
Lancashire, 73, 74, 75
Lanceley, William, 19
Lancet, 39
Landownership, 5–6, 17, 62–63
Landseer, Sir Edwin, 24
Lark Rise (Thompson), 58, 63
Law, 39, 80, **81**, 106, 108–11
Leamington, Warwickshire, 85
Leech, John, caricature by, **43**
Leeds, Yorkshire, 48, 67–68, **68–69**, 73, 86, 111, 121
Leicester Prison, 109
Leicestershire, 56
Leigh, Lady, 20
Leisure Hour, newspaper, 120
Levey sisters, **99**
Lewes Gaol, 109

Lichfield, Staffordshire, 50
Liddell, Alice, **40,** 41
Life at the Seaside (Frith), 99
Lister, Joseph, 123
Literature, 34, 35, 46, 120
Little Dorrit (Dickens), 118–19
Little Folks, magazine, 46, 120
Liverpool, Lancashire, 48, 51, 67, 69, 121
Livingstone, David, 32, **34**
Lloyd's Weekly Newspaper, 97
Londesborough Lodge, 122
London, England, 5, 13, 14, 15, **16–17,** 21–22,
    23, 25–26, **36–37,** 38, 41, 52, 58, 67, 68–
    70, 72, **73, 74, 78,** 79, 80, **81,** 81–82, 83,
    84, **84–85,** 86–87, **87,** 89, 93, 95, 96, 98,
    104, 105, 106, **106, 107,** 108, 110, 111,
    113–15, 119, 122, **124–25**
London, University of, 48
London: a Pilgrimage (Jerrold and Doré), **106,**
    107
London at Table, 86–87
Longleat, 19
Ludgate Circus, London, **78,** 79

M

Macaulay, Thomas Babington, 86
Macready, William Charles, 35
Madame Rachel's, New Bond Street, London,
    10
Manchester, Lancashire, 48, 52, 67, 70, 72, 73,
    74, 82, 83, 86, 90, 92, 106, 118, 121
Manners for Men, 31
Manufacturing. *See* Factories; Industry; Labor
Marlborough, duchess of, 5, 6–7, 20, 57
Marlborough, eighth duke of, 6
Marlborough, ninth duke of, 5, 6–7, 57
Marlborough School, 47
Marriage, 39, 113
Marryat, Captain Frederick, 46
Martin Chuzzlewit (Dickens), 82
Maurice, F. D., 48
Mayhew, Henry, 52
McAdam, John, 81
Medicine, 35, 38–39, 42, 43, 58, 122–23
Melbourne, second viscount, 14, 115
Menager, Monsieur, 21
Methodist Church, 117
Metropolitan Line, London, 82
Metropolitan Police Act, 110
Middle class, 27, **28,** 29–39, 48, 79–80, 86, 98,
    111, 113, **114,** 115, 117, 120–21
Midlands, 55
Mikado (Gilbert and Sullivan), **98**
Mill on the Floss (Eliot), 120
Millais, Sir John Everett, 13
Milner Field, Yorkshire, 14
Mines and Collieries Act, 75
Mining, **67,** 74–76, **76, 77**
Mr. Sponge's Sporting Tour (Surtees), 56
Montalbo, countess of, 15
Monte Carlo, 87
Monthly Packet, magazine, 120
More, Hannah, 41
Morning Chronicle, 89, 95
Morris, William, 24
Morton, William T. G., 123
Music, 34–35, 90, 93, 95, **98, 99, 116–17**
My Secret Life, 115

N

Naples, Italy, 52
Napoleonic Wars, 109
Newcastle-on-Tyne, Northumberland, 111, 121
Newgate Prison, 108
Nicholas Nickleby (Dickens), 51
Nightingale, Florence, **35,** 122
Nobility, 5–6, 14–17, 57, 58
Norfolk, 55
North London Collegiate School for Ladies, 48
Northumberland, duke of, 5
Nubbles, Kit, 93, 95

O

Old Curiosity Shop (Dickens), 80
Oliver Twist (Dickens), 76

Orchardleigh House, Somersetshire, 14
Osborne House, 14, 123
Ostend, Belgium, 105
Oxford University, 46, 47, 48, 100
Oxfordshire, 55

P

Paddington Station, London, **84–85,** 86
Pall Mall Gazette, 113
Paris, France, 16, 87, 105
Parliament, 39, 56, 115, 118, 122
Party-Giving on Every Scale, 30
Peabody, George, 69
Peel, Sir Robert, 110
Pentonville Prison, **103,** 108–9
Philanthropy, 69
Phillips family, 73
"Phiz" (Hablot Knight Browne), illustration by,
    81
Pickwick Papers (Dickens), 80, **81**
Pierce, criminal, 105–6
Police, 110–11
Polignac, Prince, 87
Ponsonby, Sir Frederick, 14
Portland, duke of, 15
Portman, Lord, 14
Portsmouth, Hampshire, 29
Prestwich, Lancashire, 73
Prinseps, Mrs., 22
Prisons, **103,** 106–10, **110, 111**
Prostitution, 113–15
Publisher's Circular, 120
Pückler-Muskau, Prince, 8
Pugin, Augustus Welby, 15
Punch, cartoon from, **20**
Punch and Judy show, **50**

Q

Quakers, 115
Queen's College, London, 48

R

Racing, 92, **92–93,** 99
Railroads, 34, 48, **79,** 81–86, 87, 98, 103
Ramsgate, Kent, 99
Reading Prison, 108
Recreation, 14, 32–35, **37–38,** 38, 45–46, 79–80,
    88, 89–100, **100–101,** 119, 120
    See also Sports and games
Reform Club, London, 87
Religion, 58, **112,** 113, **114,** 115, 117–20
Reynold's Weekly, newspaper, 119
Rickett, Thomas, 83
Ritchie, John, painting by, **36–37**
Ritz, César, 87
Roads, 81
Roedean School, 48
Roman Catholic Church, 115
Rome, Italy, 42
Roseberry, fifth earl of, 6
Rotten Row, London, 13, 114
Royal Academy of Art, 92, 113
Rugby School, 46–47, 115
Ruskin, Effie, 39
Ruskin, John, 13, 24, 81, 83, 120
Russell, Lady Georgiana, 122
Russell Hotel, Bloomsbury, **87**
Rutland, duke of, 9

S

Sadler's Wells Theatre, London, 93
St. Pancras Station, London, 86
St. Paul's, London, 16, **17,** 104, **124–25**
St. Thomas's Hospital, 122
Salford, Lancashire, 118
Salisbury, third marquis of, 13, 55
Salt, Sir Titus, 69, 73
Sandringham House, Norfolk, 57, 117
Sanitation, 121–22
Savoy Hotel, London, 87
Sayers, Tom, 99
Scarborough, Yorkshire, 45
Scarisbrick, Charles, 15–16
Scarisbrick Hall, Lancashire, 15–16
Scilly Isles, **64–65**

Scotland, 14, 50, 74, 100, 117, 119
Sefton, Lord, 21
Servants, 17, **18,** 19–27, 30, 45, 115
Seven Lamps of Architecture (Ruskin), 24
Shaftesbury Commission, 74–75
Shakespeare, William, 93
Shanklin, Isle of Wight, 98
Shaw, Norman, 14
Sheffield, Yorkshire, 83
Shrewsbury School, 47
Shropshire, 56, 104, 109
Simpson, Sir James, 123
Sitwell, Osbert, 45
Sitwell family, 45
Slums, **66,** 68–69, 68–70, **70, 71,** 72
Smith, Reverend Sydney, 46
Smith, Thomas Assheton, 56
Society for Promoting the External Observance
    of the Lord's Day, 120
Society for the Suppression of Public Lewdness,
    120
Society Small Talk, 32
Somersetshire, 58, 63, 121
South America, 64
South Eastern Railway Company, 105
South London Baptist Tabernacle, 117
South Western Railway, 86
Southport, Lancashire, **122**
Soyer, Alexis, 87
Spencer, Lord and Lady, 20
Sports and games, **12–13,** 32–35, 45–46, 47, 56–
    57, **88,** 89–100, 119
    See also Hunting; Recreation
Spurgeon, Reverend C. H., 117–18
Staffordshire, 16, 63, 73
Stead, W. T., 113, 114
Stephenson, George, 73
Stowe, 15
Sullivan, Arthur, 98
Summer's Day in Hyde Park (Ritchie), **36–37**
Surrey Music Hall Company, 118
Surtees, R. S., 56
Sussex, 42, 104
Sutherland, duke of, 6, 15
Sweet-Escott, Reverend Thomas, 58

T

Taine, Hippolyte Adolphe, 14, 68, 115, 119
Tayler, William, 22, 23
Tedworth, Hampshire, 56
Telford, Thomas, 81
Terry, Ellen, 10, **35**
Tess of the d'Urbervilles (Hardy), 120
Thackeray, William Makepeace, 84
Thames River, 94
Theatre, 31, 35, 90, 92–93, 95–96, **98, 99, 116–17**
Third Public Health Act, 122
Thompson, Flora, 55, 58, 63
Thring, headmaster, 47
Times, 22
Tissot, James, paintings by, **6, 11**
Tothill Fields Prison, **111**
Toys, **45,** 45–46
Tranby Croft, 14
Transportation, 34, **79,** 80–86
Travel, 81–87, 97–98, 99
Trollope, Anthony, 9, 17, 58
Two Ways of Life, photograph, **118–19**

U

United States. *See* America
Universities, 48–50
Uppingham School, 47

V

Vanderbilt, Consuelo. *See* Marlborough, duch-
    ess of
Vanderbilt, Cornelius, 6
Victoria, queen, **4,** 5, 9, 14, 15, 82, 119, 123, **124,**
    125
Victoria Station, London, 86
Victoria University, 48

W

Wales, 16, 23, 50, 73, 74, 100, 117
Walter, John, 20

Waltham, rector of, **62**
Warwickshire, 34
Water Babies (Kingsley), 42
Waterhouse, Alfred, 14
Waterloo Hotel, London, 87
Waterloo Station, London, 86
Way We Live Now (Trollope), 17
Welbeck Abbey, 15
Wellington, duke of, 82–83
Westminster, duke of, 5, 14, 16, 20, 41
Westminster, London, 56
Westminster School, 47
Weston-super-Mare, Somersetshire, 98
Wight, Isle of, 14, 98
Wilde, Oscar, 108
Willenhall, Staffordshire, 106
Willoughby de Broke, Lord, 123
Wilson, Sir Arthur, 14
Wiltshire, 58, 121
Winchester School, Hampshire, 47
Windsor Castle, 14, 82, 122
Wives and Daughters (Gaskell), 58
Wolverton, Lord, 14
Women, 10, 12, 31–32, 38–39, 48, 72, 74–76,
    112, 113, **113**
Women's rights, 39
Woodhead tunnel, 83
Woodstock, Oxfordshire, 6
Woolwich, 82
Worksop, Nottinghamshire, 15
Wright, Thomas, 90, 92–93, 103
Wyndham, George, 16

Y

Yonge, Charlotte, 42, 45, 46
Yorkshire, **57,** 69, 74, 104
Yorkshire Schools, 50–51
Young, Sir George, 46
Young Troublesome (Leech), **43**